ZOE MINISTRIES INTERNATIONAL

HOW TO HEAR GOD'S VOICE
IN MARRIAGE

FACILITATOR MANUAL

Copyright © 1997, 2015
All rights reserved.
Printed in the United States of America

This manual or parts thereof may not be reproduced, stored or transmitted in any form by any means without prior written permission of ZOE Ministries International, except as provided by United States of America copyright law.

> ZOE Ministries International
> PO Box 2207
> Arvada CO 80001-2207, USA
> permissions@zoemin.org

All scripture quotations, unless otherwise indicated, are taken from the Holy Bible, New International Version ® NIV ® Copyright © 1973, 1978, 1984 by Biblica, Inc.® Used by permission of Zondervan. All rights reserved worldwide. www.zondervan.com.

Scripture quotations marked (AMP) are taken from The Amplified Bible, Old Testament. Copyright © 1965, 1987 by The Zondervan Corporation. The Amplified New Testament, copyright © 1954, 1959, 1987 by the Lockman Foundation. Used by permission.

Scripture quotations marked (TLB) are taken from The Living Bible copyright © 1971. Used by permission of Tyndale House Publishers, Inc., Wheaton, Illinois 60189. All rights reserved.

Scripture quotations are taken from The Message Copyright © 1993 by Eugene H. Peterson. Used by permission of NavPress Publishing Group.

Quotes used by permission from Finis Jennings Dake, Sr., Author of Dake's Annotated Reference Bible.

Excerpts taken from The Blood Covenant published by Impact Books, Inc. Copyright © 1975. All Rights Reserved.

Love Is A Decision, Gary Smalley and John Trent, Ph.D., 1989, Word, Inc., Dallas, Texas. Used with permission.

"A Matter of Life and Death" from Hope of Glory Home Churches, Morrison, Colorado. Used by permission.

Quotes from *Hear Comes the Bride* are used with permission of author, Richard Booker, Bible teacher and author.

Rev. 01/20

ACKNOWLEDGEMENTS

ZOE Ministries International is dedicated to training, equipping and sending believers into the world to minister by the leading of the Holy Spirit. This ministry helps build the Body of Christ and encourages God's people to use their gifts and talents for His glory. It is for this purpose that this manual has been compiled by the leading of the Holy Spirit and the input of many people. ZOE Ministries wishes to thank them for their support, time and talents in putting this manual together. We give our Lord all the praise and glory for this work!

CONTENTS

Foreword 7

Introductory Comments to Facilitators............................. 9

Lesson 1   Introduction.. 11

Lesson 2   Growing in the Likeness of Christ............................. 25

Lesson 3   In the Beginning God Created........................ 37

Lesson 4   Covenant Relationships 55

Lesson 5   Lifetime Love Affair....................................... 63

Lesson 6   Prescription for a Superb Marriage............. 75

Lesson 7   True Romance 83

Lesson 8   Let's Communicate.. 93

Lesson 9   Let's Communicate (continued) 101

Lesson 10 Freedom Through Forgiveness 113

Lesson 11 How to Save Your Marriage Alone............ 123

Lesson 12 Serving God Together.................................. 133

Endnotes 141

Appendix A 145

Appendix B 151

> This material is designed for use within a specific format. Facilitator Training is a necessary prerequisite before this material may be used effectively in a Bible study or class setting.

ZOE MINISTRIES INTERNATIONAL

FOREWORD

Dear Facilitator,

We praise the Lord that you have been led by the Holy Spirit to facilitate a course on marriage. We believe that this is one of the most important courses offered by ZOE Ministries.

As a couple grows in their marriage, their ministry together will soon begin to blossom. The enemy is trying very hard to destroy marriages and families, for he knows the power a couple can generate when they are in agreement. **Ecclesiastes 4:12** says, **"Though one may be overpowered, two can defend themselves. A cord of three strands is not quickly broken."** When God is placed in the center of the marriage relationship, we see strength and power that the world will want to examine.

We pray that as you study this curriculum, God will truly do signs and wonders in the lives of those in this class.

God bless you, and we will be praying **Matthew 19:6, "Therefore what God has joined together, let no man separate."**

Dick and Ginny Chanda
Founding Directors

INTRODUCTORY COMMENTS
TO FACILITATORS

As an introduction to this manual, we have summarized information that we feel will be helpful to you during this course. Some of this information was covered during your facilitator training.

- DIRECTIONAL INFORMATION FOR FACILITATORS IS OUTLINED IN THIS FONT FOR QUICK IDENTIFICATION

- Remember, do not just teach this material unless you are instructed to do so in the manual. As a facilitator, you need to remember that you are a coach and you are there to encourage class participation.

- The first few lessons of this course will have a more instructional format. Some of the early lessons include teachings that provide a common base of understanding for your class members.

- If a lesson contains a teaching, please let the class know that you are teaching from the *Facilitator Manual* provided by ZOE Ministries International.

- Lessons without teachings provide you with an opportunity to model how participants should lead class discussions later in the course.

- **Facilitators should lead all the discussions in Lessons 1 through 3 and the Scripture discussions in Lessons 5, 6, 8, 9 and 12. Participants should begin leading book and article discussions in Lesson 4. You may assign a couple or class member to lead the Scripture discussion in Lessons 4, 7, 10 and 11.**

- As a facilitator, it is your responsibility to encourage the class to share the insights that God gave them as they studied the assigned material. Ask questions that will draw out these insights.

- You are not expected, nor should you attempt, to cover every point in each lesson. These points are provided for your edification and only those that directly support the main principle should be included in the class discussion.

- As participants become more involved in leading class discussions, your primary purpose is to coordinate the class and allow the Lord to build individuals' confidence and leadership abilities.

- During a class discussion, if someone's answer or insight is not scripturally correct or not related to the discussion, please do not directly address this with the individual. Instead, redirect the discussion back to the main principle of the lesson.

- **As in the Hearing God's Voice course, this course includes times of ministry specifically for the discussion leaders. In Lessons 4 through 12 the discussion leaders should receive ministry during their lesson's ministry time.**

- Remember, as a facilitator, you cannot solve each person's or couple's problems. You are to present principles from God's Word and allow the Holy Spirit to help class members apply them to their lives.

- Finally, we respectfully ask that this copyrighted material not be copied or reproduced for other purposes without express written permission of ZOE Ministries International. We request this not to "control" the material, but for two reasons: 1) Without proper facilitator training, the class will not be what we feel the Holy Spirit wants it to be, and 2) We need to honor those who have graciously given us permission to reprint or quote their materials. As stewards of their authorship, we are responsible for not using this material beyond the limitations that they have requested.

Thank you for your involvement in this ZOE course and we join you in praying that the Holy Spirit will transform participants' lives!

IN MARRIAGE

LESSON 1

INTRODUCTION

MAIN PRINCIPLE

God has a design and purpose for every marriage, and He must be central to the marriage relationship. His help and guidance are essential for any marriage to become all He has designed it to be.

LESSON 1

Introduction

I. Let's Get Started!

A. WELCOME CLASS MEMBERS.

B. OPEN WITH PRAYER. DURING TIMES OF PRAYER IN THE CLASS, YOU MIGHT ENCOURAGE COUPLES TO HOLD HANDS.

C. GET ACQUAINTED. HAVE EVERYONE TELL THEIR NAME AND SHARE SOMETHING ABOUT THEMSELVES, I.E., HOW LONG THEY HAVE BEEN MARRIED, HOW MANY CHILDREN THEY HAVE, ETC. (DON'T LET THIS LAST MORE THAN 15 MINUTES.) START WITH YOURSELF.

D. HAVE SOMEONE READ THE MAIN PRINCIPLE FOR TODAY'S LESSON.

II. Introduction to ZOE Ministries International

A. The Purpose of ZOE Ministries

Zoe is a Greek word for *life* found in many Scriptures, including **John 17:3—"Now this is eternal life: that they may know you, the only true God, and Jesus Christ, whom you have sent."** The purpose of ZOE Ministries is to bring forth *zoe*, God's vibrant life, in individual believers so that their daily lives glorify God as they minister that life to others.

Lesson 1 — Introduction

B. The Goal of ZOE Ministries

1. Our goal is to train and equip believers to make disciples, which is in keeping with the commission given to us by Jesus in **Matthew 28:19–20—"Therefore go and make disciples of all nations, baptizing them in the name of the Father and of the Son and of the Holy Spirit, and teaching them to obey everything I have commanded you. And surely I am with you always, to the very end of the age."**

2. How do we accomplish our goal of making disciples?

    a. **By training and equipping through our courses**

    - **Hearing, Knowing, and Following God's Voice Courses**—This series of 12-week discipleship courses can help us hear God's voice in various aspects of Christian life. They provide discipleship in a group setting.

    - **Discipleship by the Word of God and the Power of the Holy Spirit**—This course provides training on how to disciple individuals one-on-one, thereby allowing them to take great strides in their personal relationship with God and ministry. This method of discipleship uses the Word and the leading of the Holy Spirit as the only tools. It is changing lives in a very simple, yet powerful way.

    - **Captivated by Their Character**—To meet the need for evangelistic outreach, we have designed a home-based series of lessons. This three-part series is designed for the unbeliever, new believer, or those who need a refresher on the Trinity.

The six-week courses are:
1. Who Is Jesus?
2. Who Is God the Father?
3. Who Is the Holy Spirit?

b. **By imparting God's life**
Our mission is to impart God's life (*zoe*) into the hearts of responsive people. We desire to see that *zoe* life manifested in individual believers, so that their daily lives glorify God as they minister that life to others.

c. **By connecting the Bride of Christ (the Church) with the Bridegroom**
Our heart is to see a holy, Spirit-led bride become alive with a burning passion for our soon-coming King, Judge and Bridegroom. God has called us to do this by training the bride (the Church) to **hear**, **know** and **follow** God's voice.

IF AVAILABLE, PLEASE DISTRIBUTE ZOE MINISTRIES INTERNATIONAL BROCHURES TO THOSE INTERESTED IN MORE INFORMATION, OR REFER TO THE ZOE WEBSITE: WWW.ZOEMINISTRIES.ORG.

III. Time of Worship

(DECIDE WHETHER YOUR CLASS SHOULD TAKE TIME TO WORSHIP DURING THIS LESSON.)

SHARE THE FOLLOWING WITH THE CLASS, AS THE LORD LEADS:

There are several reasons why we take class time to worship. Besides the fact that He is worthy of our praise, worship prepares our hearts to better hear God during class. It helps us get our eyes off of ourselves and back on the Lord. Worship reminds us of God's love, faithfulness and awesome power.

IV. Introduction to This Training Course

A. The purposes of this course are:

1. To study God's Word, to learn His design and purpose for your marriage.

2. To learn His design and purpose for you as a spouse. The emphasis will be on what God is calling you to change.

    The purpose of this course is not to dwell on or discuss our spouses' faults, short-comings or sins. It is always easier to see the speck in another's eye than it is to see the log in your own eye. Please emphasize your mate's good points!

3. To be not only hearers of the Word, but doers of the Word!

4. To encourage and pray for each other.

5. It is not to give others our advice; we will be looking to God for advice and guidance.

6. To keep confidential all things said in class.

B. Course materials include:

1. Study Guide—This includes a course outline, which gives the Scripture and the book assignment for each week, as well as supporting articles.

2. Bible—any version.

3. *Love Life For Every Married Couple* by Ed Wheat, M.D.—This will be used as a textbook in this course.

4. Journal—It is highly recommended that you keep a journal during this course and write down what you hear the Lord saying to you.

V. Class Format—Lessons 2–12

A. Opening Time

This includes welcoming the class, prayer for that session, worshiping the Lord (unless in a shortened class), sharing what God has done in the previous week, and making announcements.

B. Discussion of the Book, Scripture and Articles

1. The reading assignments for each week are listed on the course outline in the Study Guide. MAKE SURE EVERYONE UNDERSTANDS WHAT THEY ARE SUPPOSED TO READ FOR LESSON 2 AND REVIEW THE MAIN PRINCIPLE FOR NEXT WEEK'S LESSON.

2. Everyone needs to come prepared to share what they learned, as the Lord leads.

3. The facilitator and assistant will lead the book, article and Scripture discussions through Lesson 3.

4. In Lessons 4, 10 and 11, one participant or couple may be asked to lead the Scripture discussion. In Lesson 4 through the end of the course, one participant or couple will be assigned to lead the book and the assigned article discussions.

5. *We cannot emphasize enough the importance of everyone asking the Holy Spirit for new insights from the Scriptures.*

C. Ministry Time

A ministry time will end each class.

D. Class Length

The length of the class is approximately $2-2\frac{1}{2}$ hours ($1\frac{1}{2}$ hours for a shortened class).

VI. Your Responsibility as a Participant

REFER THE CLASS TO THE **"PARTICIPANT'S RESPONSIBILITIES"** IN THEIR STUDY GUIDE. GO OVER THIS WITH THEM NOW.

In addition, class members should keep confidential everything that is shared during class.

VII. Discussion of the Class Article

READ THE CLASS ARTICLE LISTED FOR LESSON 1 ON YOUR COURSE OUTLINE. HAVE THE PARTICIPANTS TAKE TURNS READING A COLUMN OF THE ARTICLE. IF A CLASS MEMBER DOES NOT WISH TO READ ALOUD, HE OR SHE MAY PASS. ALLOW TIME FOR COMMENTS FROM PARTICIPANTS.

VIII. Lesson 1 Teaching

A. HAVE SOMEONE READ THE MAIN PRINCIPLE FOR THIS LESSON.

B. From its very beginning, the institution of marriage has been the God-ordained bonding of one man and one woman to become one flesh as long as both shall live. READ **GENESIS 2:21–24.**

If two people are to become one in a growing, lifelong union, God must be central to that relationship. His help and guidance are essential for a marriage to become all He has designed it to be.

C. The importance of the Lord's involvement in a marriage is illustrated by a braid. A braid appears to contain only two strands of hair or thread. But it is impossible to create a braid with only two strands. If two strands were braided together, it would quickly unravel. (YOU MAY WANT TO DEMONSTRATE BRAIDING SOMETHING.)

Lesson 1 — Introduction

> God should be the third strand—the third person—in our marriage. He can provide needed wisdom, strength or love. If we always look to God for our complete satisfaction in life, we will never be disappointed in our spouse.

So, what looks like two strands actually requires a third. The third strand, although not immediately evident, keeps the braid tightly woven. In a Christian marriage, God's presence—like the third strand in a braid—holds husband and wife together. READ **ECCLESIASTES 4:9–12**.

D. If God ever leads you to a cross-cultural mission field, you will need to keep clear in your minds God's design for your marriage. Sometimes there can be pressure to conform your marriage to that culture's marital customs. In your home you would want to be sure not to deviate from the marital roles God has laid out for you.

E. **Discuss These Questions:**

1. How would you define marriage?

2. What does the term loyalty mean to you? (One definition of loyalty is "the state of being faithful to a person, ideal or custom; feelings of devoted attachment and affection."[1])

3. How does commitment or a covenant impact a marriage?

F. **Summary of the Course**

1. As we study the Scriptures and the book, we will recognize God's blueprint for the marriage relationship

and will learn how to include God as part of our marriage.

2. We will learn what God expects of us as a husband or wife and how we can encourage and pray for our spouse.

3. We will discover how to have a lifetime love affair and how to restore romance in our marriage.

4. We will learn how to better communicate with our spouses.

5. Guidance will be provided for those who need to heal their marriage without the help of their partner.

6. So, come with expectation and a willingness to learn God's plan for us as wives or husbands. Let's be hearers of the Word and doers of the Word.

IX. Next Week's Assignment

A. REVIEW THE ASSIGNMENT LISTED ON THE COURSE OUTLINE FOR LESSON 2.

B. REVIEW THE MAIN PRINCIPLE FOR THE NEXT LESSON SO THE CLASS CAN READ THE ASSIGNMENT WITH THE PRINCIPLE IN MIND.

X. Ministry Time

A. AS FACILITATOR, YOU NEED TO GUIDE THE MINISTRY TIME. REFER TO THE "CLASS

FORMAT" SECTION OF THE *FACILITATOR TRAINING STUDY GUIDE* AND READ THE "MINISTRY TIME" SECTION.

B. DURING THE MINISTRY TIME, WE SUGGEST THAT YOU DO NOT ASK CLASS MEMBERS FOR THEIR PRAYER REQUESTS. SAY TO THE PARTICIPANTS, "In general, in this course we wait until Lesson 4 to begin personal prayer ministry. In Lessons 4-12 we will minister to each lesson's discussion leaders during their lesson's ministry time."

C. ON THE OTHER HAND, IF YOU SENSE THE LORD DIRECTING YOU TO ADDRESS THE NEED FOR PERSONAL PRAYER MINISTRY IN A CLASS MEMBER, ASK THE PERSON CONCERNED IF HE OR SHE WOULD LIKE PRAYER. INITIALLY, YOU MAY NEED TO DO THE MINISTERING, THEREBY SETTING THE EXAMPLE FOR THE CLASS.

D. THERE WILL BE VARYING DEGREES OF PROBLEMS IN THE MARRIAGES IN YOUR GROUP—SOME MORE SERIOUS THAN OTHERS. BE CAREFUL THAT MINISTRY DOES NOT GET TOTALLY FOCUSED ON ONE PERSON OR COUPLE WITH A SERIOUS PROBLEM TO THE NEGLECT OF OTHER CLASS MEMBERS. THIS COUPLE'S PROBLEMS MAY NEED TO BE ADDRESSED, BUT NOT AT THE COST OF THE WHOLE GROUP. THIS COUPLE SHOULD BE REFERRED TO A PASTOR.

E. AT THE BEGINNING OF THE MINISTRY TIME INSTRUCT THE CLASS:

Generally, we minister with our eyes open, so we can see how the person to whom we are ministering is doing. It is most important to have the compassion of the Lord when we minister, wanting solely to bless that person. Usually, only men touch men, and only women should lay hands on women. If you feel led to touch someone of the opposite sex, a hand on the back of the shoulder might be appropriate. We want to be sensitive to the person who is receiving ministry.

As we minister to each other, we need to recognize that we are all fine-tuning our hearing of God's voice. We may not hear clearly all the time, so we need to carefully weigh any word of prophecy a class member gives us. The following is a helpful guideline:

If it doesn't make sense, put it on the shelf. If it contradicts what God has told you, let it drop. If your spirit confirms it, make a note of it in your journal and watch God bring it about.

F. ENCOURAGE HANDS-ON MINISTRY BY CLASS MEMBERS. ALLOW THE GIFTS OF THE SPIRIT TO MANIFEST IN DIFFERENT PEOPLE.

G. BE CAREFUL THAT ONE PERSON DOES NOT DOMINATE THE MINISTERING.

H. CLOSE THE CLASS WITH PRAYER. A SAMPLE CLOSING PRAYER FOLLOWS:

Father, we thank You for what You have done in our lives today. We ask that by Your Holy Spirit You would seal all that was accomplished. We thank You for Your grace and mercy that enables us to walk with the Holy Spirit and to personally know Jesus. Lord, give an understanding of Your plan for each of our marriages. Help us be willing and able to put into practice what we learn from Your Word. Guard and protect us until we meet again, and give us insight about the readings assigned for next week. In Jesus' mighty name, Amen.

IN MARRIAGE

LESSON 2

GROWING IN THE LIKENESS OF CHRIST

MAIN PRINCIPLE

We need to grow in the likeness of Christ and take this likeness into our marriage. Scripture shows us how to become the kind of spouse God wants us to be. The fruit of the spirit can be manifested in us, enhancing our marriage.

WWW.ZOEMINISTRIES.ORG

LESSON 2

Growing in the Likeness of Christ

I. Let's Get Started!

A. WELCOME THE CLASS AND ENCOURAGE PARTICIPANTS TO SHARE WHAT GOD HAS BEEN DOING IN THEIR LIVES THIS PAST WEEK.

B. OPEN WITH PRAYER.

C. WORSHIP THE LORD. SHARE THE FOLLOWING WITH THE CLASS, AS THE LORD LEADS:

There are several reasons why we take class time to worship. Besides the fact that he is worthy of our praise, worship prepares our hearts to hear God better during class. It helps us get our eyes off of ourselves and back on the Lord. Worship reminds us of God's love, faithfulness and awesome power.

D. HAVE SOMEONE READ THE MAIN PRINCIPLE FOR THIS LESSON.

II. Supporting Principles From the Book

ASK THE HOLY SPIRIT TO GUIDE YOU TO THE PORTIONS OF THE BOOK ASSIGNMENT THAT ARE IMPORTANT FOR YOUR CLASS TO DISCUSS. THE MAIN PRINCIPLE FOR THE LESSON MAY AID YOU IN FINDING THE IMPORTANT POINTS. POSE QUESTIONS TO DRAW OUT INSIGHTS FROM PARTICIPANTS.

III. "Fruit of the Spirit—In Marriage" Study Help

ASK PARTICIPANTS TO RE-READ THE STUDY HELP AND INITIAL THE FRUIT THEY THINK GOD IS TELLING THEM HE WANTS TO WORK ON IN THEM. IF IT SEEMS APPROPRIATE, HAVE THEM SHARE IN CLASS WHAT THEY INITIALED.

IV. Supporting Principles From Scripture—
Philippians 2:3–4
Romans 8:1–14
Galatians 5:22–26

People want to know how to raise good children or have a healthy marriage. It all boils down to having a Christ-like attitude and Spirit-led behavior in your home day-to-day. If you are willing to be conformed to the likeness of Christ, if you are willing to be obedient to what God is telling you in your dealings with your loved ones, your family and marriage will become strong.

A. Philippians 2:3–4

We can grow in the likeness of Christ by following these admonitions and we can take this likeness of Christ into our marriages.

1. Selfishness and conceit are enemies of a marriage and hinder unity (**verse 3**). Don't oppose your spouse by acting for personal gain or from vanity.

    a. Selfishness—some people live only to please themselves, which results in seeds of discord being sown. Paul, in **Ephesians 4:2–3**, encourages working together to keep unity. The way to avoid selfishness is to make it a habit to think and act in the interest of your spouse. Be more interested in seeing God bless him or her than yourself (**verse 4**).

In **Matthew 20:28** Jesus said, **"The son of man did not come to be served, but to serve, and to give his life as a ransom for many."**

b. Conceit—being free of conceit is not thinking of yourself as a "worm" or putting yourself down. Rather, it is walking as Jesus walked (**verses 5–8**). The way to avoid conceit is to not glory in your own giftings, but to consider your spouse better than yourself. Also important is recognizing your own weaknesses, failures and limitations (**verse 3**).

B. Romans 8:1–14

READ THIS PASSAGE IN SEVERAL TRANSLATIONS, INCLUDING FROM *THE MESSAGE* FOUND IN **APPENDIX A**.

1. As we grow in the likeness of Jesus:

   a. We will make mistakes, but have no condemnation (**verse 1**)

   b. We are free from the law of sin (**verse 2**).

   c. We are free from eternal death (**verse 2**).

   d. Sin is condemned in our flesh (**verse 3**).

Lesson 2 — Growing in the Likeness of Christ

    e. We have life and peace (**verse 6**).

    f. We can live a Spirit-led life (**verses 9–11**).

    g. Our body is dead to sin (**verse 10**).

    h. Our flesh is crucified (**verses 12–13**).

    i. We walk after the Spirit and not after the flesh (**verse 14**).

2. Those who set their eyes on Jesus and who want to grow in his likeness will fulfill the things of the Spirit (**verse 5**).

3. If we *keep our eyes on Jesus* and *walk in the Spirit*, it will bring life and peace, not only in our individual lives, but also in our marriages (**verse 6**).

C. Discussion of the Article "Called To Be Christ-Like"

DRAW OUT COMMENTS ABOUT THIS ARTICLE FROM SEVERAL PEOPLE.

D. Galatians 5:22–26

1. When we desire to grow in the likeness of Christ and when we live to please God, we harvest a life and character produced in us by the Holy Spirit. Jesus has dealt with the old life and made us new. By his power, we can have victory over sin and control over the flesh (**verse 24**).

2. Compare this passage to **2 Corinthians 5:17 (AMP)**. **"Therefore if any person is [ingrafted] in Christ (the Messiah) he is a new creation (a new creature**

altogether); the old [previous moral and spiritual condition] has passed away. Behold, the fresh *and* new has come!"

Now we can act accordingly, letting his Spirit control our everyday life (**verse 25**).

3. Our marriage relationships can be transformed as we **"live in the Spirit." Verse 25** in the *King James Version* reads, **"If we live in the Spirit, let us also walk in the Spirit."**

   a. The term *live* is translated from the Greek word *zao* (dzah´-o), which can mean to have Christ living and operative in you, i.e., to have the holy mind and energy of Christ pervading and moving you.[1]

   This requires understanding how to hear, know and follow God's voice, which every child of God has the ability to do (**Romans 8:14**).

   Living in the Spirit in your marriage will have a uniqueness that only God can produce.

   ---

   b. The term *walk* is translated from the Greek word *stoicheo* (stoy-kheh´-o), which means to walk in line with, march in battle order, fall into line.[2]

   Walking in the Spirit in our marriages is the means of developing unity and harmony in our homes.

   To walk in the Spirit is to walk along a path He lays down for us.

4. As we walk in the Spirit in married life, we walk in line with the Holy Spirit, submitting our hearts to God and following his guidance.

5. We need to be aware of the pitfalls that can tempt and ensnare us and keep us from growing in Christ's likeness. These things can also prevent the transformation of our marriage relationship:

   a. Being conceited or boastful.

   b. Being competitive and challenging, provoking and irritating one another.

   c. Envying and being jealous of each other (**verse 26**).

V. Discussion of the Article "A New Heart"

ASK CLASS MEMBERS WHAT THEY THOUGHT WERE THE MOST IMPORTANT POINTS IN THIS ARTICLE.

VI. Next Week's Assignment

A. REVIEW NEXT WEEK'S ASSIGNMENT LISTED ON THE COURSE OUTLINE.

B. REVIEW THE MAIN PRINCIPLE FOR NEXT WEEK'S CLASS.

C. MAKE THE DISCUSSION LEADER ASSIGNMENTS FOR LESSON 4 EITHER NOW OR NEXT WEEK: ONE PARTICIPANT TO LEAD THE

SCRIPTURE DISCUSSION AND ANOTHER FOR THE BOOK DISCUSSION.

D. ENCOURAGE THE CLASS TO ASK GOD FOR WORDS OF ENCOURAGEMENT FOR THE DISCUSSION LEADERS. IF THIS IS NEW TO YOUR CLASS, YOU MIGHT USE THE FOLLOWING EXPLANATION:

The idea of asking God for Scripture verses or words of encouragement for someone else may be new to you. We are just taking God at His word in **Jeremiah 33:3: "Call to me and I will answer you and tell you great and unsearchable things you do not know."**

We can call on God and ask Him to give us Scripture verses or words of encouragement that He wants the discussion leaders to hear from Him. Don't be discouraged if you don't get something for each person. Your responsibility is to give God the time and opportunity to communicate with you—the rest is up to God.

NOTE:
MAKE SURE EACH COUPLE/CLASS MEMBER HAS A TURN AT LEADING A DISCUSSION DURING THE COURSE. THE CLASS SHOULD MINISTER TO THESE DISCUSSION LEADERS AT THE END OF THE LESSON THEY HAVE LED.

YOU NEED TO CALL OR VISIT THE LESSON 4 DISCUSSION LEADERS DURING THE WEEK BEFORE THAT CLASS. SEE **APPENDIX B** FOR QUESTIONS YOU CAN USE DURING THIS CONVERSATION TO HELP THE LEADER PREPARE FOR THIS CLASS. REMEMBER TO CALL

THE DISCUSSION LEADERS DURING THE WEEK BEFORE *EACH* LESSON.

VII. Ministry Time

A. AS FACILITATOR, YOU NEED TO GUIDE THE MINISTRY TIME. REFER TO THE "CLASS FORMAT" SECTION OF THE *FACILITATOR TRAINING STUDY GUIDE* AND READ THE "MINISTRY TIME" SECTION.

B. DURING THE MINISTRY TIME, WE SUGGEST THAT YOU DO NOT ASK CLASS MEMBERS FOR THEIR PRAYER REQUESTS. SAY TO THE PARTICIPANTS, "In general, in this course we wait until Lesson 4 to begin personal prayer ministry. In Lessons 4-12 we will minister to each lesson's discussion leaders during their lesson's ministry time."

C. ON THE OTHER HAND, IF YOU SENSE THE LORD DIRECTING YOU TO ADDRESS THE NEED FOR PERSONAL PRAYER MINISTRY IN A CLASS MEMBER, ASK THE PERSON CONCERNED IF HE OR SHE WOULD LIKE PRAYER. INITIALLY, YOU MAY NEED TO DO THE MINISTERING, THEREBY SETTING THE EXAMPLE FOR THE CLASS.

D. THE FOLLOWING IS REPEATED FROM LESSON 1. DEPENDING ON THE MATURITY OF YOUR CLASS AND WHETHER OR NOT NEW MEMBERS ARE PRESENT, YOU MAY ELECT TO REPEAT OR JUST PARAPHRASE THESE INSTRUCTIONS.

BEGIN BY ASKING THE PERSON IF HE OR SHE WOULD LIKE PRAYER. THEN INSTRUCT THE CLASS:

Generally, we minister with our eyes open, so we can see how the person to whom we are ministering is doing. It is most important to have the compassion of the Lord when we minister, wanting solely to bless that person. Usually, only men touch men, and only women should lay hands on women. If you feel led to touch someone of the opposite sex, a hand on the back of the shoulder might be appropriate. We want to be sensitive to the person who is receiving ministry.

As we minister to each other, we need to recognize that we are all fine-tuning our hearing of God's voice. We may not hear clearly all the time, so we need to carefully weigh any word of prophecy a class member gives us. The following is a helpful guideline:

If it doesn't make sense, put it on the shelf. If it contradicts what God has told you, let it drop. If your spirit confirms it, make a note of it in your journal and watch God bring it about.

E. ENCOURAGE HANDS-ON MINISTRY BY CLASS MEMBERS. ALLOW THE GIFTS OF THE SPIRIT TO MANIFEST IN DIFFERENT PEOPLE.

F. BE CAREFUL THAT ONE PERSON DOES NOT DOMINATE THE MINISTERING.

G. CLOSE THE CLASS WITH PRAYER A SAMPLE CLOSING PRAYER FOLLOWS:

Father, we thank you for what You have done in our lives today. We ask that by Your Holy Spirit You would seal all that was accomplished. Lord, give an understanding of Your plan for each of our marriages. Help us be willing and able to put into practice what we learn from Your Word. We thank You for Your grace and mercy that enables us to walk, exhibiting the fruit of the Spirit. Guard and protect us until we meet again, and give us insight about the readings assigned for next week. In Jesus' mighty name, Amen.

IN MARRIAGE

LESSON 3

IN THE BEGINNING GOD CREATED

MAIN PRINCIPLE

God created male and female. Each is unique, created to be different, but created for each other. God meant for man and wife to live side by side in complementary roles.

LESSON 3

In The Beginning God Created

I. Let's Get Started!

A. WELCOME THE CLASS AND ENCOURAGE PARTICIPANTS TO SHARE WHAT GOD HAS BEEN DOING IN THEIR LIVES THIS PAST WEEK.

B. OPEN WITH PRAYER.

C. WORSHIP THE LORD. SHARE THE FOLLOWING WITH THE CLASS, AS THE LORD LEADS:

There are several reasons why we take class time to worship. Besides the fact that He is worthy of our praise, worship prepares our hearts to hear God better during class. It helps us get our eyes off ourselves and back on the Lord. Worship reminds us of God's love, faithfulness and awesome power.

D. HAVE SOMEONE READ THE MAIN PRINCIPLE FOR THIS LESSON.

II. Supporting Principles From the Book

ASK THE HOLY SPIRIT TO GUIDE YOU TO THE PORTIONS OF THE BOOK ASSIGNMENT THAT ARE IMPORTANT FOR YOUR CLASS TO DISCUSS. THE MAIN PRINCIPLE FOR THE LESSON MAY AID YOU IN FINDING THE IMPORTANT POINTS. POSE QUESTIONS TO DRAW OUT INSIGHTS FROM PARTICIPANTS.

III. Discussion of the Article "Undivided: God's Plan For Couples In The Ministry"

ASK CLASS MEMBERS WHAT THEY THOUGHT WERE THE MOST IMPORTANT POINTS IN THIS ARTICLE.

IV. Supporting Principles From Scripture—Genesis 1:1–2, 26–28 Genesis 2:7, 18–25

THE FOLLOWING MATERIAL WILL NEED TO BE PRESENTED AS A TEACHING.

A. Introduction

In the beginning God created the heavens and the earth and God saw that it was good. God created the perfect environment for mankind before He made man. The word created is *bara* (baw-raw´) in Hebrew, which means to create something out of nothing.[1]

B. READ GENESIS 1:1–2, 26–28

1. **"Then God said, 'Let us make man in our image...' " Genesis 1:26.** *Us* refers to the Trinity—God the Father, the Son and the Holy Spirit. Each Person of the Trinity was present at creation.

    a. Here God is translated *Elohim* (eh-lo´-heem), which means "the Almighty God, Creator" and indicates a plurality of three or more.[2] The Lord Almighty (*Jehovah*) made the earth by His power, wisdom and understanding (**Jeremiah 51:15**).

b. READ **JOHN 1:2–3**. All things were made through Jesus, who was with God the Father in the beginning.

c. In **Genesis 1:2** the action of the Holy Spirit at creation is translated as "to brood."[3] A mother hen broods when she sits on her eggs to hatch them and later covers her young with her wings. The Holy Spirit's personality is nurturing and protective.

2. The Hebrew word for *man* in **verses 26–27** is *adam* (aw-dawm´), which means mankind or human being and includes both male and female.[4] **"When God created man, he made him in the likeness of God. He created them male and female and blessed them. And when they were created, he called them 'man' "** Genesis 5:1–2.

3. Both male and female were given dominion over creation (**verse 26**).

4. Both received God's blessing (**verse 28**).

C. READ GENESIS 2:7, 18–25.

1. **"Then the Lord God formed man from the dust of the ground and breathed into his nostrils the breath or spirit of life, and man became a living being" Genesis 2:7 (AMP).**

   The verb *formed* is *jatsar* (yaw-tsar´) in Hebrew and means to mold or shape something like a lump of clay.[5] **"Let us make man in our image..." Genesis 1:26.** The verb *make* is *asah* (aw-saw´) in Hebrew, which means "to manufacture something out of something."[6] So, man was manufactured by God out of the existing soil by molding and shaping him.

"Because man's body was formed from the dust of the ground, because it was made out of something which already existed [soil], his body was *asah*-made. But the spirit of the man was *bara*-created. The spirit of man had no origin, and it was not made out of anything that previously existed. God created the spirit of man."[7]

When a person is conceived in the womb, his body is made from existing material, the egg and sperm. But his spirit is created (*bara*) at the moment of conception supernaturally by God.[8]

2. **"Now the Lord God said, 'It is not good (sufficient, satisfactory) that the man should be alone; I will make him a helper meet (suitable, adapted, complementary) for him' " Genesis 2:18 (AMP).**

   a. It was not good for the man to be without the companionship of someone like himself.

   b. "Man was not complete and could not reproduce his kind alone . . . ."[9]

   c. The woman was to be "a help suitable to man: intellectually, morally and physically—as his counterpart."[10] *Meet* in Hebrew translates as "aid or help; surround, protect . . . ."[11]

3. **"And the Lord God caused a deep sleep to fall upon Adam; and while he slept, He took one of**

his ribs or a part of his side and closed up the [place with] flesh" Genesis 2:21 (AMP).

"Woman is said not to have been taken out of man's head to be lorded-over by him, nor from his feet to be trampled on by him, but from his side to be equal with him, from under his arm to be protected by him, and from near his heart to be loved by him."[12]

4. **"And the rib *or* part of his side which the Lord God had taken from the man he built up *and* made into a woman, and he brought her to the man" Genesis 2:22 (AMP).**

   a. ". . . God made the woman in an entirely different manner than He made the man or any other creature."[13]

   According to Bob Yandian in his book *One Flesh*:

   In this verse, we have a different word from *asah* (to make something from something), *bara* (to create something from nothing), and *jatsar* (to mold, shape or form something). The Hebrew word translated **made** here is *bana* (baw-naw´), which means "to build something."

   God took the rib in His hands and supernaturally multiplied it and constructed it into the body of the woman. Just like the loaves and fishes multiplied in the hands of Jesus (**John 6:5–14**), God multiplied the rib and built it, piece by piece, into the form of Eve. The man and all the other creatures were molded from the dust of the ground, but the woman was *built*. (We still use that term today!)[14]

b. *He* in **verse 22** refers to the Father.[15] Just as a father brings his daughter to the groom during the wedding ceremony, so God the Father brought the woman, His special, unique creation, to the man.

5. **"This is now bone of my bones and flesh of my flesh; she shall be called 'woman,' for she was taken out of man" Genesis 2:23.**

The man rejoiced about being given this wonderful companion.

6. **"For this reason a man shall leave his father and mother and be united to his wife, and they will become one flesh" Genesis 2:24.**

   a. To *be united* to comes from the Hebrew word *proskollao* (pros-kol-lah´-o), which means to adhere, abide fast, to cleave fast together, or to stick.[16] This word indicates fidelity and permanency in a relationship. **Matthew 19:4–6** speaks of this inseparable union.

///
All other relationships should be secondary when husband and wife are united with each other.
///

   b. This one flesh relationship is also mentioned in **Ephesians 5:31**, and is likened to the relationship between Christ and the Church.

D. **Comparisons**

"They [priests] serve at a sanctuary that is a copy [type] and shadow of what is in heaven" Hebrews 8:5.

1. We can find similarities between the husband's role and that of Christ, and between the wife's role and that of the Holy Spirit.

    a. Man is a type of Christ.

        Ephesians 5:23a, 25 "For the husband is the head of the wife as Christ is the head of the church . . . Husbands, love your wives, just as Christ loved the church and gave himself up for her . . .."

The husband is the spiritual leader of the family. He should love as Jesus did, with unconditional love.

        "A husband is to love as Jesus loves. That means to love, protect, and provide for his wife . . . Jesus supplies all of our needs because He has a heart to give, not because we are perfect all the time . . . Jesus is the husband's example, and the Church, which He is sanctifying and cleansing through His Word, is not perfect . . . Yet, Jesus continues to love, protect, and instruct us to the degree we will allow Him!"[17]

The husband lays down his life for his family. Like Jesus, the husband is obedient to God the Father and he puts the needs of his family before his own needs.

    b. Woman is a type of the Holy Spirit.

        - There is not a specific verse that *directly* correlates the role of the wife with the role of the Holy Spirit, but similarities can be seen by comparing the following verses:

Lesson 3 — In The Beginning God Created

"The Lord God said, 'It is not good for the man to be alone . . .' " **Genesis 2:18a.**

In **John 14:18 (AMP)** Jesus talked to his disciples about sending the Holy Spirit: **"I will not leave you as orphans [comfortless, desolate, bereaved, forlorn, helpless] . . .."**

- Compare these two verses also:

". . . I will make a helper suitable for him" **Genesis 2:18.** *The Amplified Bible* reads, **"I will make him a helper meet (suitable, adapted, complementary) for him.' "**

Remember the Hebrew definitions of *meet* are aid, help, surround and protect.

"And I will ask the Father, and He will give you another Comforter (Counselor, Helper, Intercessor, Advocate, Strengthener, and Standby), that He may remain with you forever . . ." John 14:16 (AMP).

The wife should aid, comfort, counsel and provide support for her husband. She is called to come alongside and help.

2. The marriage union is like the indwelling of the Holy Spirit.

Compare these verses:

"For this reason a man will leave his father and

mother and be united to his wife, and they will become one flesh" Genesis 2:24.

In **John 14:17b (AMP)** Jesus said, **"He [the Holy Spirit] lives with you [constantly] and will be in you."**

Both the indwelling of the Holy Spirit and the marriage union are intended to be permanent.

3. The attitude of the persons of the Trinity toward each other is a pattern for marriage partners to follow.

   a. Jesus' attitude towards the Holy Spirit is like the attitude a husband should have toward his wife.

   In **Mark 3:29 (AMP)** Jesus said, **"But whoever speaks abusively against or maliciously misrepresents the Holy Spirit can never get forgiveness, but is guilty of and is in the grasp of an everlasting trespass."**

   Paul agreed in **Ephesians 4:30 (AMP): "And do not grieve the Holy Spirit of God [do not offend or vex or sadden Him]...."** The Holy Spirit is referred to in a protective way.

The husband's attitude should be that of protecting and caring for his wife.

   Part of the reason Jesus willingly laid down His life was so that the Holy Spirit could come to earth and bring about the creation of children of God (**Romans 8:15–16**).

The husband should be willing to lay down his life and care for his family, so that healthy children can be raised.

b. The Holy Spirit's attitude towards Jesus is like the attitude a wife should have towards her husband.

"When the counselor comes, whom I will send to you from the Father, the Spirit of truth who goes out from the Father, he will testify about me" John 15:26.

"He will not speak on his own; he will speak only what he hears, and he will tell you what is yet to come. He will bring glory to me by taking from what is mine and making it known to you" John 16:13b–14.

A wife should be eager to tell others about her husband's good qualities. A wife's attitude should be one of honor and respect toward her husband.

The Holy Spirit always points to Jesus and gives Him glory and honor. The Holy Spirit loves Jesus and wants to see Him exalted. **Ephesians 5:33** says **"The wife must respect her husband."** Respect means "to be in awe of, to revere."[18]

4. Just as each person of the Trinity has specific functions, so the partners of a marriage have

individual roles. When a husband or wife is not fulfilling their God-given role, you will find a family that is functioning at a below optimum level and isn't exhibiting God's love in the world.

Picture a marriage as a triangle with God the Father as the apex. On either end of the base are the husband, the type of Christ, and the wife, the type of the Holy Spirit.

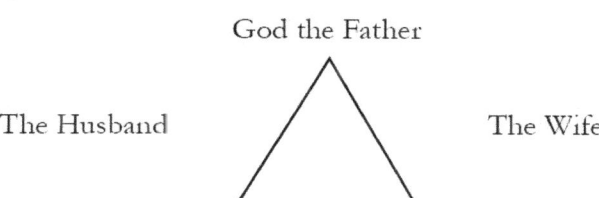

God's role is to provide all we need to be successful in our marriages. *He is eager to speak to us, giving us guidance on how to love our spouse.* Ideally, the husband loves, protects, cares for and lays down his life for his wife; while the wife loves, respects, defends and offers help, comfort and godly counsel to her husband. A husband and wife can ask God the Father for what they need in their marriage, e.g., love, wisdom, or strength. The closer we draw to God, the closer we are drawn to one another.

Jesus and the Holy Spirit never compete or act independently of each other. READ **ACTS 10:38**. They have always worked together to do good for God the Father and to bring glory to Him. So the husband and wife should work together in a complementary fashion.

God did not give this teaching so that we could say, "I'm like Jesus!" or "I'm like the Holy Spirit!", but so that we could more clearly see God's design for us and, thereby, bring glory to the Father.

V. Discussion of the Article "Guess What... God Knows Best"

ASK CLASS MEMBERS WHAT THEY THOUGHT WERE THE MOST IMPORTANT POINTS IN THIS ARTICLE.

VI. Next Week's Assignment

A. REVIEW NEXT WEEK'S ASSIGNMENT LISTED ON THE COURSE OUTLINE.

B. REVIEW THE MAIN PRINCIPLE FOR NEXT WEEK'S CLASS.

C. ASSIGN A COUPLE/CLASS MEMBER TO LEAD THE BOOK AND ARTICLE DISCUSSIONS FOR LESSON 5 EITHER NOW OR NEXT WEEK. ASK THE CLASS TO PRAY FOR THEM AS THEY PREPARE TO LEAD THE DISCUSSIONS.

D. THE SCRIPTURE ASSIGNMENT FOR LESSON 5 DEALS WITH SEXUALITY. GENERALLY, THE FACILITATOR LEADS THIS DISCUSSION DUE TO THE SENSITIVE NATURE OF THIS SUBJECT, BUT USE YOUR JUDGMENT.

E. ENCOURAGE THE CLASS TO ASK GOD DURING THE WEEK FOR A SCRIPTURE OR A WORD OF

ENCOURAGEMENT OR EXHORTATION FOR NEXT WEEK'S DISCUSSION LEADERS AND TO BRING IT TO CLASS. TELL THEM THAT NEXT WEEK'S LESSON INCLUDES A TIME OF PRAYER AND MINISTRY FOR THIS COUPLE/PERSON.

IF THIS IS NEW TO YOUR CLASS, YOU MIGHT USE THE FOLLOWING EXPLANATION:

The idea of asking God for Scripture verses or words of encouragement for someone else may be new to you. We are just taking God at His word in **Jeremiah 33:3: "Call to me and I will answer you and tell you great and unsearchable things you do not know."**

We can call on God and ask Him to give us Scripture verses or words of encouragement that He wants the discussion leaders to hear from Him. Don't be discouraged if you don't get something for each person. Your responsibility is to give God the time and opportunity to communicate with you—the rest is up to God.

NOTE:
YOU NEED TO CALL OR VISIT THE LESSON 4 DISCUSSION LEADERS DURING THE WEEK BEFORE THAT CLASS. SEE **APPENDIX B** FOR QUESTIONS YOU CAN USE DURING THIS CONVERSATION TO HELP THE LEADER PREPARE FOR THIS CLASS. REMEMBER TO CALL THE DISCUSSION LEADERS DURING THE WEEK BEFORE ***EACH*** LESSON.

VII. Ministry Time

A. AS FACILITATOR, YOU NEED TO GUIDE THE MINISTRY TIME. REFER TO THE "CLASS FORMAT" SECTION OF THE FACILITATOR TRAINING STUDY GUIDE AND READ THE "MINISTRY TIME" SECTION. (Note: The *Facilitator Training Study Guide* is the book you received during Facilitator Training.)

B. DURING THE MINISTRY TIME, WE SUGGEST THAT YOU DO NOT ASK CLASS MEMBERS FOR THEIR PRAYER REQUESTS. SAY TO THE PARTICIPANTS, "In general, in this course we wait until Lesson 4 to begin personal prayer ministry. In Lessons 4-12 we will minister to each lesson's discussion leaders during their lesson's ministry time."

C. ON THE OTHER HAND, IF YOU SENSE THE LORD DIRECTING YOU TO ADDRESS THE NEED FOR PERSONAL PRAYER MINISTRY IN A CLASS MEMBER, ASK THE PERSON CONCERNED IF HE OR SHE WOULD LIKE PRAYER. INITIALLY, YOU MAY NEED TO DO THE MINISTERING, THEREBY SETTING THE EXAMPLE FOR THE CLASS.

D. THERE WILL BE VARYING DEGREES OF PROBLEMS IN THE MARRIAGES IN YOUR GROUP—SOME MORE SERIOUS THAN OTHERS. BE CAREFUL THAT MINISTRY DOES NOT GET TOTALLY FOCUSED ON ONE PERSON OR COUPLE WITH A SERIOUS PROBLEM TO THE NEGLECT OF OTHER CLASS MEMBERS. THIS COUPLE'S PROBLEMS MAY NEED TO BE

ADDRESSED, BUT NOT AT THE COST OF THE WHOLE GROUP. THIS COUPLE SHOULD BE REFERRED TO A PASTOR.

E. THE FOLLOWING IS REPEATED FROM LESSON 1. DEPENDING ON THE MATURITY OF YOUR CLASS AND WHETHER OR NOT NEW MEMBERS ARE PRESENT, YOU MAY ELECT TO REPEAT OR JUST PARAPHRASE THESE INSTRUCTIONS.

BEGIN BY ASKING THE PERSON IF HE OR SHE WOULD LIKE PRAYER. THEN INSTRUCT THE CLASS:

Generally, we minister with our eyes open, so we can see how the person to whom we are ministering is doing. It is most important to have the compassion of the Lord when we minister, wanting solely to bless that person. Usually, only men touch men, and only women should lay hands on women. If you feel led to touch someone of the opposite sex, a hand on the back of the shoulder might be appropriate. We want to be sensitive to the person who is receiving ministry.

As we minister to each other, we need to recognize that we are all fine-tuning our hearing of God's voice. We may not hear clearly all the time, so we need to carefully weigh any word of prophecy a class member gives us. The following is a helpful guideline:

If it doesn't make sense, put it on the shelf. If it contradicts what God has told you, let it drop. If your spirit confirms it, make a note of it in your journal and watch God bring it about.

F. ENCOURAGE HANDS-ON MINISTRY BY CLASS MEMBERS. ALLOW THE GIFTS OF THE SPIRIT TO MANIFEST IN DIFFERENT PEOPLE.

G. BE CAREFUL THAT ONE PERSON DOES NOT DOMINATE THE MINISTERING.

H. CLOSE THE CLASS WITH PRAYER. (See sample prayer in Lesson 2.)

IN MARRIAGE

LESSON 4

COVENANT RELATIONSHIPS

MAIN PRINCIPLE

A covenant is a permanent agreement involving the total being of the persons concerned. When we marry we form a blood covenant with our mate in the eyes of God. Marriage is a covenant relationship that brings with it all the benefits and responsibilities of a blood covenant.

WWW.ZOEMINISTRIES.ORG

LESSON 4

Covenant Relationships

I. Let's Get Started!

A. WELCOME THE CLASS AND ENCOURAGE PARTICIPANTS TO SHARE WHAT GOD HAS BEEN DOING IN THEIR LIVES THIS PAST WEEK.

B. OPEN WITH PRAYER.

C. WORSHIP THE LORD.

D. HAVE SOMEONE READ THE MAIN PRINCIPLE FOR TODAY'S LESSON.

II. Supporting Principles From the Book

ENCOURAGE THE DISCUSSION LEADER AND PARTICIPANTS TO FOCUS ON PORTIONS OF THE BOOK ASSIGNMENT THAT ARE IMPORTANT FOR THIS CLASS TO DISCUSS, ESPECIALLY AS IT RELATES TO THE MAIN PRINCIPLE.

III. Supporting Principles From Scripture—The Book of Hosea; Wheat, pages 228–236

ENCOURAGE THE DISCUSSION LEADER AND PARTICIPANTS TO FOCUS ON PORTIONS OF THE SCRIPTURE ASSIGNMENT THAT ARE IMPORTANT

Lesson 4 — Covenant Relationships

FOR THIS CLASS TO DISCUSS, ESPECIALLY AS IT RELATES TO THE MAIN PRINCIPLE.

A. Hosea gives the ultimate blueprint for an unconditional love—love without limits—which eventually reunites husband and wife in spite of tremendous obstacles.

B. We see two relationships in the book of **Hosea**. One is God and His people Israel and the other is a husband and wife.

1. God commanded Hosea to take a wife—Gomer, a woman God knew would prove unfaithful. She was a prostitute. God made this unusual request in order to illustrate the infidelity of His covenant people. The nation of Israel had been unfaithful to God as they worshiped false gods.

2. This was the true condition of Israel. They were prostituting themselves to idols. God had called Israel, married her, and brought her into covenant relationship as His people.

3. After having her third child, Gomer left Hosea to pursue old lovers. God commanded Hosea to buy her back as his wife and to make a contract that she would never again pursue her former lovers.

   Hosea's experience was used to teach Israel that she would have to return to God after forsaking His covenant and worshiping other gods. God would "marry" her again and enter into an eternal covenant relationship with her.

C. Hosea's experience made the way so plain. However, Hosea's contemporaries ignored this lesson, that is, until the Assyrians came and destroyed their splendid capital, Samaria, and took the remaining Israelites into exile.

D. Hosea's experience can help us to determine, with God's help, to have unconditional love. We need to be willing to forsake everything to restore a marriage.

Hosea's experience gives us hope and encouragement that a marriage can be healed and restored in spite of tremendous obstacles.

IV. Discussion of the Study Help "Covenant Relationships"

ENCOURAGE THE DISCUSSION LEADER AND PARTICIPANTS TO FOCUS ON PORTIONS OF THE STUDY HELP THAT ARE IMPORTANT FOR THIS CLASS TO DISCUSS, ESPECIALLY AS IT RELATES TO THE MAIN PRINCIPLE.

V. Next Week's Assignment

A. REVIEW NEXT WEEK'S ASSIGNMENT LISTED ON THE COURSE OUTLINE.

B. REVIEW THE MAIN PRINCIPLE FOR NEXT WEEK'S LESSON.

C. ASSIGN A COUPLE/PARTICIPANT TO LEAD THE BOOK AND ARTICLE DISCUSSIONS FOR LESSON 6. ASK THE CLASS TO PRAY FOR THEM AS THEY PREPARE TO LEAD THE DISCUSSIONS.

D. THE SCRIPTURE ASSIGNMENT FOR LESSON 6 DISCUSSES SEXUALITY, A SENSITIVE SUBJECT FOR SOME. GENERALLY, THE FACILITATOR LEADS THIS CLASS, BUT USE YOUR JUDGMENT ACCORDING TO PARTICIPANTS' ABILITIES.

E. ENCOURAGE THE CLASS TO ASK GOD DURING THE WEEK FOR A SCRIPTURE OR A WORD OF ENCOURAGEMENT OR EXHORTATION FOR NEXT WEEK'S DISCUSSION LEADERS AND TO BRING IT TO CLASS. TELL THEM THAT NEXT WEEK'S LESSON INCLUDES A TIME OF PRAYER AND MINISTRY FOR THIS COUPLE/PERSON.

NOTE TO THE FACILITATOR:
YOU NEED TO CALL OR VISIT THE LESSON 5 DISCUSSION LEADERS DURING THE WEEK BEFORE THAT CLASS. SEE **APPENDIX B** FOR QUESTIONS YOU CAN USE DURING THIS CONVERSATION TO HELP THE LEADER PREPARE FOR THIS CLASS. REMEMBER TO CALL THE DISCUSSION LEADERS DURING THE WEEK BEFORE ***EACH*** LESSON.

VI. Ministry Time

A. AS FACILITATOR, YOU NEED TO GUIDE THE MINISTRY TIME. REFER TO THE "CLASS FORMAT" SECTION OF THE *FACILITATOR TRAINING STUDY GUIDE* AND READ THE "MINISTRY TIME" SECTION. (NOTE: The *Facilitator Training Study Guide* is the book you received during Facilitator Training.)

B. BE SURE TO PRAY FOR THIS WEEK'S DISCUSSION LEADERS. ENCOURAGE PARTICIPANTS TO SHARE ANY SCRIPTURES OR WORDS OF ENCOURAGEMENT THAT THE LORD GAVE FOR THESE LEADERS.

C. NOTE: THE MINISTRY EMPHASIS HAS NOW SHIFTED TO THE WEEKLY DISCUSSION LEADERS. ANY OTHER PERSONAL MINISTRY SHOULD NOW BE ADDRESSED AFTER CLASS UNLESS THE HOLY SPIRIT STRONGLY DIRECTS YOU OTHERWISE.

D. THE FOLLOWING IS REPEATED FROM LESSON 1. DEPENDING ON THE MATURITY OF YOUR CLASS AND WHETHER OR NOT NEW MEMBERS ARE PRESENT, YOU MAY ELECT TO REPEAT OR JUST PARAPHRASE THESE INSTRUCTIONS.

BEGIN BY ASKING THE PERSON IF HE OR SHE WOULD LIKE PRAYER. THEN INSTRUCT THE CLASS:

Generally, we minister with our eyes open, so we can see how the person to whom we are ministering is doing. It is most important to have the compassion of the Lord when we minister, wanting solely to bless that person. Usually, only men touch men, and only women should lay hands on women. If you feel led to touch someone of the opposite sex, a hand on the back of the shoulder might be appropriate. We want to be sensitive to the person who is receiving ministry.

As we minister to each other, we need to recognize that we are all fine-tuning our hearing of God's voice. We may not hear clearly all the time, so we need to carefully weigh any word of prophecy a class member gives us. The following is a helpful guideline:

If it doesn't make sense, put it on the shelf. If it contradicts what God has told you, let it drop. If your spirit confirms it, make a note of it in your journal and watch God bring it about.

E. ENCOURAGE HANDS-ON MINISTRY BY CLASS MEMBERS. ALLOW THE GIFTS OF THE SPIRIT TO MANIFEST IN DIFFERENT PEOPLE.

F. BE CAREFUL THAT ONE PERSON DOES NOT DOMINATE THE MINISTERING.

G. CLOSE THE CLASS WITH PRAYER (See sample prayer in Lesson 2.)

IN MARRIAGE

LESSON 5

LIFETIME LOVE AFFAIR

MAIN PRINCIPLE

In order for us to have a lifetime love affair with our mate, we need all five aspects of love to be evident in our marriage. We must love, respect and care for our mate's body as much as we love, respect and care for our own body. As these principles are practiced in our marriage, we can remain faithful to one another.

WWW.ZOEMINISTRIES.ORG

LESSON 5

Lifetime Love Affair

I. Let's Get Started!

A. WELCOME THE CLASS AND ENCOURAGE PARTICIPANTS TO SHARE WHAT GOD HAS BEEN DOING IN THEIR LIVES THIS PAST WEEK.

B. OPEN WITH PRAYER.

C. WORSHIP THE LORD.

D. HAVE SOMEONE READ THE MAIN PRINCIPLE FOR TODAY'S LESSON.

II. Five Greatest Needs In Marriage Exercise

If we are to have a lifetime love affair, then we really ought to know our spouses' needs. Today we'll do an exercise that will show us how well we know our mates.

REFER PARTICIPANTS TO THE <u>TWO COPIES</u> OF THE CLASS WORKSHEET **"FIVE GREATEST NEEDS IN MARRIAGE."** HAVE EACH CLASS MEMBER WRITE DOWN HIS OR HER FIVE GREATEST NEEDS IN MARRIAGE. THEN HAVE EACH WRITE DOWN WHAT HE OR SHE THINKS ARE HIS OR HER MATE'S FIVE GREATEST NEEDS. MARRIAGE PARTNERS ARE NOT TO CONFER ON THIS—EACH IS TO FILL IT OUT INDEPENDENTLY. THESE WILL BE LOOKED AT AGAIN AT THE END OF THE CLASS.

III. Supporting Principles From the Book

ENCOURAGE THE DISCUSSION LEADER AND PARTICIPANTS TO FOCUS ON PORTIONS OF THE BOOK ASSIGNMENT THAT ARE IMPORTANT FOR THIS CLASS TO DISCUSS, ESPECIALLY AS IT RELATES TO THE MAIN PRINCIPLE.

IV. Supporting Principles From Scripture—
Psalm 45
Proverbs 5:15–20
1 Corinthians 7:3–5

SECTION IV. IS USUALLY LED BY THE FACILITATOR, BUT USE YOUR JUDGMENT REGARDING APTITUDE OF PARTICIPANTS.

BECAUSE THE FATHER SEES OUR SEXUALITY AS IMPORTANT, BEAUTIFUL AND SACRED, HE IS READY WITH SUGGESTIONS FOR POSITIVE CHANGE. AS YOU LEAD THIS DISCUSSION, BE VERY SENSITIVE TO THE DIRECTION OF THE HOLY SPIRIT. ALLOW YOUR CLASS THE FREEDOM TO DISCUSS THE ISSUES OF SEXUAL EXPRESSION IN MARRIAGE. HOWEVER, IF A PARTICIPANT'S COMMENT IS CONDEMNING IN SOME WAY, STOP BRIEFLY AND PRAY ALOUD FOR GUIDANCE IN THE DISCUSSION. RECOMMEND DR. WHEAT'S BOOK *INTENDED FOR PLEASURE* TO THOSE WHO WOULD LIKE FURTHER SPECIFIC INFORMATION.

A. Jewish Wedding Customs[1]

A traditional Jewish wedding began when the groom brought a marriage contract and a bride price to the bride and her father for approval. If they accepted them, the couple was betrothed. This meant they were legally married, although they were not yet ready or able to live together as husband and wife. During the period of time between the betrothal and the wedding ceremony, the groom built a bridal chamber in his father's house and the bride prepared herself for married life.

When the groom finished preparing the bridal chamber, he and his friends proceeded to the bride's house, blowing a ram's horn to announce their coming. They then whisked the bride and her friends away to the groom's house with much noise and frivolity. When the bride and groom arrived at the groom's house, they were ushered into the specially prepared bridal chamber. The marriage was consummated through sexual union while the guests waited outside. As a proof of virginity and *the sealing of the blood covenant of marriage*, a blood-stained honeymoon sheet was exhibited.

Once the marriage was consummated, the wedding guests celebrated with music, singing, dancing and feasting. The celebration lasted for a week while the couple honeymooned in the bridal chamber. When the bride and groom emerged a week later, everyone congratulated them and they were honored at a marriage supper.

B. Psalm 45

In *The New International Version* this psalm is called "A Wedding Song." It is about Solomon's marriage to

Pharaoh's daughter. It is also a description of Jesus by God the Father (**Hebrews 1:8–9**).

1. The king (the groom) is described as excellent, gracious and blessed (**verse 2**).

2. **Verses 3–5** tell of the power, majesty and righteousness of the king.

3. **"Gird your sword"** is an expression showing him to be capable of commanding an army[2] (**verse 3**).

4. The king's glory and majesty are something to behold by even those accustomed to splendor (**verse 4**).

5. The king is a champion of truth, humility, righteousness and justice (**verses 4, 6–7**).

6. Godly advice is given to the bride. She is to make her relationship with her husband more important than any other relationship. She is to honor and respect him as her lord (**verses 10–11**).

7. The favorable attributes of both the bride and groom are recognized and celebrated (**verses 8–13**).

8. There is great joy and celebration associated with the sexual union in marriage (**verses 14–15**).

C. **Proverbs 5:15–20**

What advice can be found here for married men?

1. Find pleasure and refreshment in your own spouse and be true to her (**verse 15**).

2. Should you have children that you won't even know about? (**verse 16**). Confine yourself to your own wife. Then there will never be any thought about a child that you fathered but have not raised. There will not be questions like "Where is my child?" or "How is he doing?" (**verse 17**).

This is a good model for us because we should "accentuate the positive" and avoid criticizing our mates.

3. Be blessed with the rewards of fidelity and rejoice with the wife of your youth. The wife of your youth should be the same wife with you in your old age (**verse 18**).

4. See the tenderness, gentleness and attractiveness of your wife and always be captivated by her love (**verse 19**).

D. 1 Corinthians 7:3–5

What advice can be found here for married Christians?

1. The husband and wife must respect each other regarding sexual needs, mutually satisfying each other (**verses 3–4**).

The bodies of a husband and wife belong to each other. Neither of them has the right to refuse the needs of their spouse.

2. Any abstention must be temporary, mutually agreed upon, and have a spiritual objective. If they do not obey this injunction, one may be responsible for the infidelity of the other (**verse 5**).

YOU MAY ALSO WANT TO READ **1 CORINTHIANS 7:1–5** FROM *THE MESSAGE* FOUND IN **APPENDIX A**.

3. Bob Yandian in his book, *One Flesh*, warns us about infrequent lovemaking.

   This verse [1 Cor. 7:5] tells how important sex is in the marriage relationship. Married couples should experience physical intimacy regularly and frequently. God commands this because it keeps your relationship healthy and strong. One of the signs that your priorities are falling out of line, or trouble has crept into your relationship, is a lack of sexual intimacy and pleasure in sex.

   Again, we can see a parallel to your relationship with the Lord. When your priorities are in line and you are keeping your heart pure before Him, you have no problem worshiping the Lord face to face. But you know your life is out of balance or you have given place to sin when it is hard to look Jesus in the eye and tell Him you love Him.

   Intimately praising and worshiping the Lord brings strength and stability to your life and acts as a safeguard to keep you on the right path. Likewise, the intimacy of making love with your spouse brings strength and stability into your marriage, and is a key factor to keeping your relationship on the right track.[3]

V. Discussion of the Assigned Article

TIME PERMITTING, ENCOURAGE THE DISCUSSION LEADER AND PARTICIPANTS TO FOCUS ON

PORTIONS OF THE ARTICLE ASSIGNMENT THAT ARE IMPORTANT FOR THIS CLASS TO DISCUSS, ESPECIALLY AS IT RELATES TO THE MAIN PRINCIPLE.

VI. A Second Look at the "Five Greatest Needs in Marriage"

HAVE THE CLASS MEMBERS LOOK AGAIN AT THEIR **"FIVE GREATEST NEEDS IN MARRIAGE"** LISTS. ALLOW THEM TO MAKE ANY CHANGES THEY WANT.

IF BOTH MARRIAGE PARTNERS ARE PRESENT, HAVE THEM SHARE THEIR LISTS WITH EACH OTHER. IF YOUR GROUP DOES NOT HAVE BOTH MARRIAGE PARTNERS IN IT, ENCOURAGE CLASS MEMBERS TO ASK THEIR SPOUSES AT HOME ABOUT THEIR FIVE GREATEST NEEDS IN MARRIAGE.

VII. Next Week's Assignment

A. REVIEW NEXT WEEK'S ASSIGNMENT LISTED ON THE COURSE OUTLINE.

MENTION TO PARTICIPANTS THAT, IF POSSIBLE, THEY SHOULD READ **SONG OF SONGS** TOGETHER, USING THE SAME TRANSLATION, PREFERABLY *THE NEW INTERNATIONAL VERSION*.

B. REVIEW THE MAIN PRINCIPLE FOR NEXT WEEK'S LESSON.

C. MAKE DISCUSSION LEADER ASSIGNMENTS FOR LESSON 7: ONE COUPLE/CLASS MEMBER FOR THE SCRIPTURE DISCUSSION AND ANOTHER TO LEAD THE BOOK AND ASSIGNED ARTICLE DISCUSSIONS. ASK THE CLASS TO PRAY FOR THEM AS THEY PREPARE TO LEAD THE DISCUSSIONS.

D. ENCOURAGE THE CLASS TO ASK GOD DURING THE WEEK FOR A SCRIPTURE OR A WORD OF ENCOURAGEMENT OR EXHORTATION FOR NEXT WEEK'S DISCUSSION LEADERS AND TO BRING IT TO CLASS. TELL THEM THAT NEXT WEEK'S LESSON INCLUDES A TIME OF PRAYER AND MINISTRY FOR THIS COUPLE/PERSON.

NOTE TO THE FACILITATOR:
YOU NEED TO CALL OR VISIT THE LESSON 6 DISCUSSION LEADERS DURING THE WEEK BEFORE THAT CLASS. SEE **APPENDIX B** FOR QUESTIONS YOU CAN USE DURING THESE CONVERSATIONS TO HELP THE LEADER PREPARE FOR THIS CLASS. REMEMBER TO CALL THE DISCUSSION LEADERS DURING THE WEEK BEFORE ***EACH*** LESSON.

VIII. Ministry Time

A. AS FACILITATOR, YOU NEED TO GUIDE THE MINISTRY TIME.

How To Hear God's Voice—In Marriage

B. BE SURE TO PRAY FOR THIS WEEK'S DISCUSSION LEADERS.

C. NOTE: THE MINISTRY EMPHASIS HAS NOW SHIFTED TO THE WEEKLY DISCUSSION LEADERS. ANY OTHER PERSONAL MINISTRY SHOULD NOW BE ADDRESSED AFTER CLASS UNLESS THE HOLY SPIRIT STRONGLY DIRECTS YOU OTHERWISE.

D. AT THE BEGINNING OF THE MINISTRY TIME REMIND PARTICIPANTS ABOUT THE FOLLOWING:

As we minister to each other, we need to recognize that we are all fine-tuning our hearing of God's voice. We may not hear clearly all the time, so we need to carefully weigh any word of prophecy a class member gives us. The following is a helpful guideline:

If it doesn't make sense, put it on the shelf. If it contradicts what God has told you, let it drop. If your spirit confirms it, make a note of it in your journal and watch God bring it about.

E. ENCOURAGE HANDS-ON MINISTRY BY CLASS MEMBERS. ALLOW THE GIFTS OF THE SPIRIT TO MANIFEST IN DIFFERENT PEOPLE.

F. BE CAREFUL THAT ONE PERSON DOES NOT DOMINATE THE MINISTERING.

G. CLOSE WITH PRAYER

IN MARRIAGE

LESSON 6

PRESCRIPTION FOR A SUPERB MARRIAGE

MAIN PRINCIPLE

God intends that a husband and wife should enjoy sexual union within the guidelines He has given. As we choose to act and think lovingly towards our mate, trust and understanding deepens, enhancing our love relationship.

WWW.ZOEMINISTRIES.ORG

LESSON 6

Prescription For A Superb Marriage

I. Let's Get Started!

   A. WELCOME THE CLASS AND ENCOURAGE PARTICIPANTS TO SHARE WHAT GOD HAS BEEN DOING IN THEIR LIVES THIS PAST WEEK.

   B. OPEN WITH PRAYER.

   C. WORSHIP THE LORD.

   D. HAVE SOMEONE READ THE MAIN PRINCIPLE FOR TODAY'S LESSON.

II. Supporting Principles From the Book

   ENCOURAGE THE DISCUSSION LEADER AND PARTICIPANTS TO FOCUS ON PORTIONS OF THE BOOK ASSIGNMENT THAT ARE IMPORTANT FOR THIS CLASS TO DISCUSS, ESPECIALLY AS IT RELATES TO THE MAIN PRINCIPLE.

III. Supporting Principles From Scripture— Song of Songs, Chapters 1–8

   A. **Song of Songs**, also known as **Song of the Solomon**, is thought to have been written by Solomon, King of Israel. The book includes a series of reflections from the perspective of a woman as she looks at her marriage.

Some commentaries say that she was Solomon's queen. She was called Shulamith, after the region from which she came.

The speeches and events don't follow a chronological order. There are several flashbacks in the story. The writer used a chorus, an imaginary group that interrupts certain scenes, to make brief speeches or give warnings. The chorus was also used to provide transitions from one scene to another or to emphasize a point.

B. Song of Solomon gives practical information we can use today. Before her wedding, Shulamith had pleasant thoughts of her future husband, anticipating sexual intercourse with him on their wedding night. She was not afraid of sex and she did not have any preconceived ideas that sex was dirty, sinful or hurtful. She had a "holy desire" for her husband.

The great message of Song of Solomon is the beauty and wonder of human sexual love as experienced within the bonds of marriage.

The sexual and physical side of marriage is a natural and proper part of God's plan. This is the same truth so evident at creation, as recorded in **Genesis 2:24–25—"For this reason a man will leave his father and mother and be united to his wife, and they shall become one flesh. The man and his wife were both naked, and they felt no shame."**

C. SOS 1:3 ". . . Your name is like perfume poured out." One of the Hebrew connotations of *name* is that it represents the person's character. Shulamith's physical desire for her husband was increased as she considered the positive aspects of his character.[1]

We become more attractive to our mate when we exhibit increasing strength of character and Christ-likeness.

D. In **chapters 1–4** of **Song of Solomon** we see the beauty of youthful and passionate love. In **chapters 5–8** we see the reality of married life. The Bible is honest, frank and realistic. It doesn't leave us with an idealized and unrealistic picture of the couple living happily ever after.

There are problems that arise and adjustments that must be made if two people are to learn to live together in a successful marriage. We need to listen for God's guidance on what adjustments to make.

E. We see a major problem that affected this couple in the early years of their marriage. Because of his job, Solomon was away from Shulamith more than she liked. He would come home late at night, when Shulamith was already in bed asleep and he would want to be intimate. Shulamith would display a lack of interest in sex and would reject his advances (**SOS 5:1–6**).

Their solution to the problem involved assuming personal responsibility for shortcomings rather than focusing on and blaming the other person. Instead of dwelling on Solomon's thoughtlessness in approaching her late at night, Shulamith began to work on her own attitude. Instead of thinking how selfish Shulamith was in rejecting him, Solomon concentrated on loving her unconditionally and blessing his wife in spite of her rejection.

F. To solve any problem in a marriage, both partners need to follow the pattern of realizing their own shortcomings and trying to change their own negative attitudes. It does no good to continually resent our mates for their faults. We need to consider our mates—their feelings, needs, desires—and to love them unconditionally.

We need to be responsible for our own attitudes and actions and allow God to deal with our mates' offending behavior.

IV. Discussion of the Assigned Article

ENCOURAGE THE DISCUSSION LEADER AND PARTICIPANTS TO FOCUS ON PORTIONS OF THE ARTICLE ASSIGNMENT THAT ARE IMPORTANT FOR THIS CLASS TO DISCUSS, ESPECIALLY AS IT RELATES TO THE MAIN PRINCIPLE.

V. Next Week's Assignment

A. REVIEW NEXT WEEK'S ASSIGNMENT LISTED ON THE CLASS OUTLINE.

B. REVIEW THE MAIN PRINCIPLE FOR NEXT WEEK'S LESSON.

C. ASSIGN A COUPLE/CLASS MEMBER TO LEAD THE BOOK AND ARTICLE DISCUSSIONS FOR LESSON 8. ASK THE CLASS TO PRAY FOR THEM AS THEY PREPARE TO LEAD THE DISCUSSIONS.

D. ENCOURAGE THE CLASS TO ASK GOD DURING THE WEEK FOR A SCRIPTURE OR A WORD OF ENCOURAGEMENT OR EXHORTATION FOR NEXT WEEK'S DISCUSSION LEADERS AND TO BRING IT TO CLASS. TELL THEM THAT NEXT WEEK'S LESSON INCLUDES A TIME OF PRAYER AND MINISTRY FOR THIS COUPLE/PERSON.

VI. Ministry Time

A. AS FACILITATOR, YOU NEED TO GUIDE THE MINISTRY TIME.

B. BE SURE TO PRAY FOR THIS WEEK'S DISCUSSION LEADERS.

C. NOTE: THE MINISTRY EMPHASIS HAS NOW SHIFTED TO THE WEEKLY DISCUSSION LEADERS. ANY OTHER PERSONAL MINISTRY SHOULD NOW BE ADDRESSED AFTER CLASS UNLESS THE HOLY SPIRIT STRONGLY DIRECTS YOU OTHERWISE.

D. AT THE BEGINNING OF THE MINISTRY TIME REMIND PARTICIPANTS ABOUT THE FOLLOWING:

As we minister to each other, we need to recognize that we are all fine-tuning our hearing of God's voice. We may not hear clearly all the time, so we need to carefully weigh any word of prophecy a class member gives us. The following is a helpful guideline:

If it doesn't make sense, put it on the shelf. If it contradicts what God has told you, let it drop. If your spirit confirms it, make a note of it in your journal and watch God bring it about.

E. ENCOURAGE HANDS-ON MINISTRY BY CLASS MEMBERS. ALLOW THE GIFTS OF THE SPIRIT TO MANIFEST IN DIFFERENT PEOPLE.

F. BE CAREFUL THAT ONE PERSON DOES NOT DOMINATE THE MINISTERING.

G. CLOSE WITH PRAYER

IN MARRIAGE

LESSON 7

TRUE ROMANCE

MAIN PRINCIPLE

There can be true romance in our marriage no matter how long or short a time we have been married. We can learn how to restore or improve the romance in our marriage.

WWW.ZOEMINISTRIES.ORG

LESSON 7

True Romance

I. Let's Get Started!

    A. WELCOME THE CLASS.

    B. OPEN WITH PRAYER.

    C. WORSHIP THE LORD.

    D. HAVE SOMEONE READ THE MAIN PRINCIPLE FOR TODAY'S LESSON.

II. Supporting Principles From the Book

ENCOURAGE THE DISCUSSION LEADER AND PARTICIPANTS TO FOCUS ON PORTIONS OF THE BOOK ASSIGNMENT THAT ARE IMPORTANT FOR THIS CLASS TO DISCUSS, ESPECIALLY AS IT RELATES TO THE MAIN PRINCIPLE.

III. Supporting Principles From Scripture—Ephesians 5

ENCOURAGE THE DISCUSSION LEADER AND PARTICIPANTS TO FOCUS ON PORTIONS OF THE SCRIPTURE ASSIGNMENT THAT ARE IMPORTANT FOR THIS CLASS TO DISCUSS, ESPECIALLY AS IT RELATES TO THE MAIN PRINCIPLE.

Lesson 7 — True Romance

In this chapter we see four different sections:

A. Live a Life of Love (verses 1–7)

B. Live as Children of Light (verses 8–14)

C. Live Wisely (verses 15–20)

D. Marriage—Christ and the Church (verses 21–33)

ASK THE CLASS: What advice in these verses could help bring the intimacy needed to foster romance in your marriage?

A. Live a Life of Love—Ephesians 5:1–7

1. Imitate God as children imitate their parents. Imitate Jesus' actions, words, nature and ways; copy His character. As we imitate Him, we walk in love and romantic love flourishes (**verse 1**).

2. Compare **verse 2** with **1 John 3:16—"this is how we know what love is: Jesus Christ laid down his life for us. And we ought to lay down our lives for our brothers."** Husband and wife walk in love when they willingly lay down their life for each other.

3. What are some examples of laying down your life in the marriage setting?

    It could mean relinquishing your expectations of what your partner should be or do. It can mean giving of your time, energy, support or possessions for your spouse.

4. As we know and receive Jesus' love for us, we are able

to love others (**1 John 4:19**) (**verse 2**).

5. As we walk in love, we will avoid sexual immorality, impurity, greed, obscenity, foolish talk and course joking. Rather than do these things, we voice our thankfulness to God for who He is and what He has done for us (**verses 3–4**).

B. Live as Children of Light—Ephesians 5:8–14

1. Once we invite Jesus into our lives, we become **"light in the lord."** We have to choose to live **"as children of light"** and avoid former **"deeds of darkness"** (**verse 8**).

    When your spouse is involved in sin, you should not participate in that sin with him or her (**verse 11**).

2. Our actions should reflect the fruits of goodness, righteousness and truth (**verse 9**). **Matthew 5:16** encourages us to: **"Let your light shine before men, that they may see your good deeds and praise your Father in heaven."**

3. Just as we should find out what pleases our mate, so we should discover what pleases God in our marriage. Let your life be a constant example of what is most acceptable to Him (**verse 10**).

4. It pleases God when you turn to Him for guidance on how to relate with your spouse.

5. **John 8:12 says, "Whoever follows me will never walk in darkness, but will have the light of life."** As we follow Jesus, we please the Father. Jesus only did what the Father told Him to do (**John 12:49– 50**). In one situation Jesus expressed righteous anger at sin; in

another He extended nonjudgmental forgiveness to a person caught in sin.

When your spouse is involved in sin, you need to ask God what you are to do in each specific situation.

C. Walk in Wisdom—Ephesians 5:15–20

1. In *The Amplified Bible* **verse 15** reads, **"Look carefully then how you walk! Live purposefully and worthily and accurately, not as the unwise and witless, but as wise (sensible, intelligent people) . . .."**

2. He admonishes us to understand and firmly grasp what the will of the Lord is. It is important to ask God for wisdom as we relate to our spouses. The only way to be truly wise is to live moment by moment according to God's will (**verse 17**).

3. To walk in wisdom is to not get drunk with wine, but rather to be continually filled and inspired by the Holy Spirit (**verse 18**).

4. Being filled and guided by the Spirit and filling our mind with God's Word brings not only wisdom, but also great joy as we fellowship with God and other believers (**verse 19**).

5. We should thank God for our partners (**verse 20**).

D. Marriage—Christ and the Church—Ephesians 5:21–33

1. Submit to each other out of respect for Christ (**verse 21**).

What does it mean to submit to each other?

Submitting to each other may mean setting aside your plans or your ideas. Is it more important to be loving or to be right? It may mean putting the interests of your mate before your own.

2. The wife should give her husband respect and loyalty. She should be submissive and adapt herself to her husband as a service to the Lord (**verses 22, 24, 33 AMP**).

READ **PROVERBS 31:12 (AMP)**—**"She comforts, encourages, and does him only good as long as there is life within her."**

3. The Christian husband should actively care for his wife with unselfish and undemanding love (**verses 23, 25, 33**).

4. The close physical bond between husband and wife is an illustration of Jesus' spiritual oneness with His Body, the Church (**verses 30–32**).

READ **EPHESIANS 5:21–33** FROM *THE MESSAGE* FOUND IN **APPENDIX A**.

As we walk in the love, light and life of Jesus, we will see intimacy increase and, along with it, romance. As we honor one another and submit to each other, we will see God working His plan and purpose in our marriage.

IV. Discussion of the Assigned Articles

TIME PERMITTING, ENCOURAGE THE DISCUSSION LEADER AND PARTICIPANTS TO FOCUS ON PORTIONS OF THE ARTICLE ASSIGNMENT THAT ARE IMPORTANT FOR THIS CLASS TO DISCUSS, ESPECIALLY AS IT RELATES TO THE MAIN PRINCIPLE.

V. Next Week's Assignment

A. REVIEW NEXT WEEK'S ASSIGNMENT LISTED ON THE COURSE OUTLINE.

B. REVIEW THE MAIN PRINCIPLE FOR NEXT WEEK'S LESSON.

C. ASSIGN A COUPLE/CLASS MEMBER TO LEAD THE BOOK AND ARTICLE DISCUSSIONS FOR LESSON 9. ASK THE CLASS TO PRAY FOR THEM AS THEY PREPARE TO LEAD THE DISCUSSIONS.

D. ENCOURAGE THE CLASS TO ASK GOD DURING THE WEEK FOR A SCRIPTURE OR A WORD OF ENCOURAGEMENT OR EXHORTATION FOR NEXT WEEK'S DISCUSSION LEADERS AND TO BRING IT TO CLASS. TELL THEM THAT NEXT WEEK'S LESSON INCLUDES A TIME OF PRAYER AND MINISTRY FOR THIS COUPLE/PERSON.

VI. Ministry Time

A. AS FACILITATOR, YOU NEED TO GUIDE THE MINISTRY TIME.

B. BE SURE TO PRAY FOR THIS WEEK'S DISCUSSION LEADERS.

C. NOTE: THE MINISTRY EMPHASIS HAS NOW SHIFTED TO THE WEEKLY DISCUSSION LEADERS. ANY OTHER PERSONAL MINISTRY SHOULD NOW BE ADDRESSED AFTER CLASS UNLESS THE HOLY SPIRIT STRONGLY DIRECTS YOU OTHERWISE.

D. AT THE BEGINNING OF THE MINISTRY TIME REMIND PARTICIPANTS ABOUT THE FOLLOWING:

As we minister to each other, we need to recognize that we are all fine-tuning our hearing of God's voice. We may not hear clearly all the time, so we need to carefully weigh any word of prophecy a class member gives us. The following is a helpful guideline:

If it doesn't make sense, put it on the shelf. If it contradicts what God has told you, let it drop. If your spirit confirms it, make a note of it in your journal and watch God bring it about.

E. ENCOURAGE HANDS-ON MINISTRY BY CLASS MEMBERS. ALLOW THE GIFTS OF THE SPIRIT TO MANIFEST IN DIFFERENT PEOPLE.

F. BE CAREFUL THAT ONE PERSON DOES NOT DOMINATE THE MINISTERING.

G. CLOSE WITH PRAYER

IN MARRIAGE

LESSON 8

LET'S COMMUNICATE

MAIN PRINCIPLE

Scripture provides a warning against the evil of an uncontrolled and uncharitable tongue. Our words can either tear down our mate or bless them and build them up. We need to communicate storge *and* phileo *love in our marriage.*

WWW.ZOEMINISTRIES.ORG

LESSON 8

Let's Communicate

I. Let's Get Started!

A. WELCOME THE CLASS AND ENCOURAGE PARTICIPANTS TO SHARE WHAT GOD HAS BEEN DOING IN THEIR LIVES IN THE PAST WEEK

B. OPEN WITH PRAYER.

C. WORSHIP THE LORD.

D. HAVE SOMEONE READ THE MAIN PRINCIPLE FOR TODAY'S LESSON.

II. Supporting Principles From the Book

ENCOURAGE THE DISCUSSION LEADER AND PARTICIPANTS TO FOCUS ON PORTIONS OF THE BOOK ASSIGNMENT THAT ARE IMPORTANT FOR THIS CLASS TO DISCUSS, ESPECIALLY AS IT RELATES TO THE MAIN PRINCIPLE.

III. Supporting Principles From Scripture—
James 3:1–12
Matthew 12:33-37

Words can be so destructive—wrecking character, reputation and relationships, undoing years of working to establish *phileo* love. By one careless, venomous, inflammatory remark we can unleash forces we are powerless to stop. What is said can never be unsaid.

A. James 3:1–12

1. **James** says that if someone never says the wrong things, he is a perfect person, able to control his whole body. Unfortunately, most of us have trouble controlling our speech (**verse 2**).

2. A horse's actions are governed by a small bit placed in its mouth. If a horse has not learned to respond to the bit, it is unruly. The tongue must be bridled so that it won't govern our actions (**verses 3–5**)

3. The tongue is a fire that can contaminate and deprave the whole body. It is like a tiny spark setting ablaze a great forest that may burn for days and go on smoldering for weeks. Speech can be dangerous; its effects can run unchecked. A whisper of gossip can set a church ablaze or inflame a city (**verse 6**).

4. Mankind can tame wild animals, but only with the power of the Holy Spirit can we subdue our tongue (**verse 8**).

5. It is not pleasing to God when with one breath we praise Him and with the next breath curse another child of God (**verses 9–10**).

6. **James** asks questions which give us food for thought. The tongue reveals the condition of the heart (**verses 11–12**).

B. Matthew 12:33-37

1. Jesus said that spoken words are the overflow of the heart. What does that say about us if the words coming out of our mouths are evil or destructive? What do we do in this case?

2. Jesus was quite clear in saying that we each will be held accountable on the day of judgment for every word we say while alive. This is a sobering thought!

3. HAVE THE CLASS TURN TO THEIR CLASS WORKSHEET **"A MATTER OF LIFE AND DEATH."**

    This study will help us become more aware of our words and the areas where we speak "life" and "death."

    What is an example of speaking "life" and "death"?

    (For example, a father would be speaking life to his daughter if he said something positive like, "Cathy, I am so proud of your good grades at school." He would be speaking death if he said something negative like, "Cathy, no man is going to marry an egghead like you.")

    As you fill it out, ask God to reveal specific times your speech was death-producing.

    HAVE EACH CLASS MEMBER FILL THIS OUT NOW.

4. AFTER THE CLASS WORKSHEET HAS BEEN COMPLETED, READ **GALATIANS 6:7-9**.

    "A man reaps what he sows" (Galatians 6:7b).

> *If you are sowing words of death into a situation, that is what you will reap. If you are sowing words of life into a situation, you will reap life.*

IV. Discussion of the Assigned Article

ENCOURAGE THE DISCUSSION LEADER AND PARTICIPANTS TO FOCUS ON PORTIONS OF THE ARTICLE ASSIGNMENT THAT ARE IMPORTANT FOR THIS CLASS TO DISCUSS, ESPECIALLY AS IT RELATES TO THE MAIN PRINCIPLE.

V. Next Week's Assignment

A. REVIEW NEXT WEEK'S ASSIGNMENT LISTED ON THE COURSE OUTLINE.

B. ASK PARTICIPANTS TO IDENTIFY THE MAIN IDEAS FROM THE SCRIPTURES ON THE STUDY HELP **"TAMING THE TONGUE."**

C. REVIEW THE MAIN PRINCIPLE FOR NEXT WEEK'S LESSON.

D. MAKE DISCUSSION LEADER ASSIGNMENTS FOR LESSON 10: ONE COUPLE/CLASS MEMBER FOR THE SCRIPTURE DISCUSSION AND ANOTHER TO LEAD THE BOOK AND ASSIGNED ARTICLE DISCUSSIONS. ASK THE CLASS TO PRAY FOR THEM AS THEY PREPARE TO LEAD THE DISCUSSIONS.

E. ENCOURAGE THE CLASS TO ASK GOD DURING THE WEEK FOR A SCRIPTURE OR A WORD OF ENCOURAGEMENT OR EXHORTATION FOR NEXT WEEK'S DISCUSSION LEADERS AND TO BRING IT TO CLASS. TELL THEM THAT NEXT WEEK'S LESSON INCLUDES A TIME OF PRAYER AND MINISTRY FOR THIS COUPLE/PERSON.

VI. Ministry Time

A. AS FACILITATOR, YOU NEED TO GUIDE THE MINISTRY TIME.

B. BE SURE TO PRAY FOR THIS WEEK'S DISCUSSION LEADERS.

C. NOTE: THE MINISTRY EMPHASIS HAS NOW SHIFTED TO THE WEEKLY DISCUSSION LEADERS. ANY OTHER PERSONAL MINISTRY SHOULD NOW BE ADDRESSED AFTER CLASS UNLESS THE HOLY SPIRIT STRONGLY DIRECTS YOU OTHERWISE.

D. AT THE BEGINNING OF THE MINISTRY TIME REMIND PARTICIPANTS ABOUT THE FOLLOWING:

As we minister to each other, we need to recognize that we are all fine-tuning our hearing of God's voice. We may not hear clearly all the time, so we need to carefully weigh any word of prophecy a class member gives us. The following is a helpful guideline:

If it doesn't make sense, put it on the shelf. If it contradicts what God has told you, let it drop. If your spirit confirms it, make a note of it in your journal and watch God bring it about.

E. ENCOURAGE HANDS-ON MINISTRY BY CLASS MEMBERS. ALLOW THE GIFTS OF THE SPIRIT TO MANIFEST IN DIFFERENT PEOPLE.

F. BE CAREFUL THAT ONE PERSON DOES NOT DOMINATE THE MINISTERING.

G. CLOSE WITH PRAYER

IN MARRIAGE

LESSON 9

LET'S COMMUNICATE (CONTINUED)

MAIN PRINCIPLE

Scripture provides a warning against the evil of an uncontrolled and uncharitable tongue. Our words can either tear down our mate or bless them and build them up. We need to communicate agape *love in our marriage.*

WWW.ZOEMINISTRIES.ORG

LESSON 9

Let's Communicate (Continued)

I. Let's Get Started!

   A. WELCOME THE CLASS AND ENCOURAGE PARTICIPANTS TO SHARE WHAT GOD HAS BEEN DOING IN THEIR LIVES IN THE PAST WEEK.

   B. OPEN WITH PRAYER.

   C. WORSHIP THE LORD.

   D. HAVE SOMEONE READ THE MAIN PRINCIPLE FOR TODAY'S LESSON.

II. Supporting Principles From the Book

   ENCOURAGE THE DISCUSSION LEADER AND PARTICIPANTS TO FOCUS ON PORTIONS OF THE BOOK ASSIGNMENT THAT ARE IMPORTANT FOR THIS CLASS TO DISCUSS, ESPECIALLY AS IT RELATES TO THE MAIN PRINCIPLE.

III. Supporting Principles From Scripture—Proverbs 18:21 "Taming The Tongue"

   A. Proverbs 18:21 (AMP)

Lesson 9 — Let's Communicate (continued)

"Death and life are in the power of the tongue, and they who indulge in it shall eat the fruit of it [for life or death]."

Have you seen this principle illustrated in your life?

What has the Lord been saying to you this past week about your words?

B. Discussion of the "Taming the Tongue" Study Help

BECAUSE THERE IS SO MUCH MATERIAL FOR THIS LESSON, BRIEFLY DISCUSS ONE OR TWO SCRIPTURES FROM EACH SECTION OF THE STUDY HELP. ASK WHICH VERSES IMPACTED PARTICIPANTS THE MOST.

1. **Results of an Out-of-Control Tongue**

    a. **Proverbs 12:18–19** and **Galatians 5:15**—Hurting people around you

    b. **Proverbs 15:4**—Crushing someone's spirit

    c. **Proverbs 25:23 (AMP)**—Causing others to be angry

    d. **Proverbs 17:20**—Falling into trouble

    e. **Proverbs 10:19**—Producing sin in your life

    f. **Matthew 15:18**—Being unclean in God's eyes

    g. **Jeremiah 9:3–9** and **Matthew 12:36–37**—Incurring God's judgment

2. **How to Tame the Tongue**

    a. **Deuteronomy 30:19–20a**—Choose life

    b. **Isaiah 30:15**—Repent

    c. **Luke 6:45** and **Ezekiel 18:30–32**—Get a new heart. The tongue can not be tamed until the heart is changed.

    | **Psalm 119:11** | |
    | **Proverbs 4:20–24** | Read, meditate on and |
    | **Hebrews 4:12–13** | memorize God's Word. |

    | **Psalm 19:14** | |
    | **Psalm 86:11** | Ask God in prayer for a new heart |
    | **Psalm 141:3** | and control of your speech. |

    | **1 Thessalonians 5:16–18** | Choose to express |
    | **Philippians 4:4–7** | gratitude and rejoice in the Lord. |

    d. **Proverbs 15:4**—Ask, "Will what I want to say build up or tear down my spouse?" Be watchful.

    e. **Exodus 14:14 "The Lord will fight for you; you need only to be still."** Sacrifice. If what you were going to say is destructive, give it up.

3. **Results of a Spirit-Controlled Tongue**

    a. **Proverbs 21:23**—Protection from calamity

    b. **Psalm 126:1–3**—A grateful and joyful life

Lesson 9 — Let's Communicate (continued)

c. **Psalm 40:9–10**—Praise for God, which can direct people around you toward Him

d. **Proverbs 12:25**—The ability to cheer up your spouse

e. **Psalm 49:3**—Wisdom that helps your family

f. **Proverbs 12:18**—Healing for your mate through wise words

g. **1 Corinthians 14:3**—Strength, encouragement and comfort for your spouse through a prophetic word

h. **Isaiah 50:4**—Help for your spouse when he/she is weary

i. **Numbers 6:22–27**—Blessings from God for your spouse

j. **Psalm 34:12–13**—Days filled with life and goodness

We can speak respectful, kind things to our mate. We can tell them that we love them and are proud of them. We can encourage them and help build up their self-esteem. We can inspire courage, boldness for the Lord, mercy and goodness in them by what we say to them.

IV. "Let's Communicate"

HAVE CLASS MEMBERS EXAMINE COMMON COMMUNICATION BLUNDERS BY ROLE-PLAYING

THE SAMPLE ARGUMENTS IN THE CLASS ROLE PLAY ENTITLED **"LET'S COMMUNICATE."** ASSIGN EACH CONVERSATION TO A COUPLE OR SET OF TWO PARTICIPANTS AND HAVE THEM ROLE PLAY THE CONVERSATIONS FOR THE CLASS.

V. Non-Verbal Communication

A. READ THE FOLLOWING STORY TO THE CLASS.

Bill and Mary accept a dinner invitation from Joe and Nancy. On the eve of the occasion the two couples enjoy a delicious meal together and then retire to the living room for conversation and relaxation.

About 10:30 p.m., Mary is anxious to go home. She glances at her husband. As she does so, she points at her watch. Bill ignores her gesture. He and Joe become so involved in a discussion about the management problems at the shop that they forget about the time.

Midnight arrives! By now, Mary is clearing her throat, tapping an impatient toe on the living room floor, and darting looks at her husband that would scorch a heat-shield. At 1:00 a.m., Bill suggests that it is time to go. As he and Mary depart the home of their hosts, he takes Mary's arm to escort her. She resists his long-delayed chivalry, darts ahead of him and into the car.

Bill, who has now caught the full impact of his wife's mood, is angered by her pouting. As much of a child as his wife, he leaps into the auto, slams the door, grinds the motor to a start and roars out of the driveway as if he

Lesson 9 — Let's Communicate (continued)

were on an emergency run. THE TWO RIDE HOME IN SILENCE!

Though no words passed between Bill and Mary from 10:30 p.m. to 1:00 a.m., each was communicating messages which, when read by the other, were as plain and clear as if they had been printed in large black letters.

B. ASK THE CLASS TO IDENTIFY THE MESSAGES THAT WERE SENT WITHOUT WORDS.

1. A gesture and the ignoring of that gesture

2. Bill's preoccupation with plant problems

3. Mary's throat-clearing, toe-tapping and "killing looks"

4. Bill's touch

5. Mary's resistance to that touch

6. Her accelerated pace to the car

7. Her husband's door-slamming and rapid exit from the driveway

8. The stony silence of both

All these non-verbal messages were like telegrams that conveyed bad news to their recipients. The incident described alerts us to the fact that *communication is more than words.* Just keeping your mouth shut is not acceptable if your heart is wrong toward your spouse.

C. On the positive side, non-verbal messages can be sent which communicate your love to your mate.

ASK THE CLASS TO CITE SOME EXAMPLES.

Examples could include the wink of an eye, the squeeze of a hand, a knowing look, etc.

VI. Next Week's Assignment

A. REVIEW NEXT WEEK'S ASSIGNMENT LISTED ON THE COURSE OUTLINE.

B. REVIEW THE MAIN PRINCIPLE FOR NEXT WEEK'S LESSON.

C. MAKE DISCUSSION LEADER ASSIGNMENTS FOR LESSON 11: ONE COUPLE/CLASS MEMBER FOR THE SCRIPTURE DISCUSSION AND ANOTHER TO LEAD THE BOOK AND ASSIGNED ARTICLE DISCUSSIONS. ASK THE CLASS TO PRAY FOR THEM AS THEY PREPARE TO LEAD THE DISCUSSIONS.

D. ENCOURAGE THE CLASS TO ASK GOD DURING THE WEEK FOR A SCRIPTURE OR A WORD OF ENCOURAGEMENT OR EXHORTATION FOR NEXT WEEK'S DISCUSSION LEADERS AND TO BRING IT TO CLASS. TELL THEM THAT NEXT WEEK'S LESSON INCLUDES A TIME OF PRAYER AND MINISTRY FOR THIS COUPLE/PERSON.

Lesson 9 — Let's Communicate (continued)

VII. Ministry Time

A. AS FACILITATOR, YOU NEED TO GUIDE THE MINISTRY TIME.

B. BE SURE TO PRAY FOR THIS WEEK'S DISCUSSION LEADERS.

C. NOTE: THE MINISTRY EMPHASIS HAS NOW SHIFTED TO THE WEEKLY DISCUSSION LEADERS. ANY OTHER PERSONAL MINISTRY SHOULD NOW BE ADDRESSED AFTER CLASS UNLESS THE HOLY SPIRIT STRONGLY DIRECTS YOU OTHERWISE.

D. AT THE BEGINNING OF THE MINISTRY TIME REMIND PARTICIPANTS ABOUT THE FOLLOWING:

As we minister to each other, we need to recognize that we are all fine-tuning our hearing of God's voice. We may not hear clearly all the time, so we need to carefully weigh any word of prophecy a class member gives us. The following is a helpful guideline:

If it doesn't make sense, put it on the shelf. If it contradicts what God has told you, let it drop. If your spirit confirms it, make a note of it in your journal and watch God bring it about.

E. ENCOURAGE HANDS-ON MINISTRY BY CLASS MEMBERS. ALLOW THE GIFTS OF THE SPIRIT TO MANIFEST IN DIFFERENT PEOPLE.

F. BE CAREFUL THAT ONE PERSON DOES NOT DOMINATE THE MINISTERING.

G. CLOSE WITH PRAYER

IN MARRIAGE

LESSON 10

FREEDOM THROUGH FORGIVENESS

MAIN PRINCIPLE

Forgiveness heals the marital relationship and frees us to establish a loving, healthy marriage.

WWW.ZOEMINISTRIES.ORG

LESSON 10

Freedom Through Forgiveness

I. Let's Get Started!

A. WELCOME THE CLASS AND ENCOURAGE PARTICIPANTS TO SHARE WHAT GOD HAS BEEN DOING IN THEIR LIVES IN THE PAST WEEK.

B. OPEN WITH PRAYER.

C. WORSHIP THE LORD.

D. HAVE SOMEONE READ THE MAIN PRINCIPLE FOR TODAY'S LESSON.

II. Supporting Principles From the Book

ENCOURAGE THE DISCUSSION LEADER AND PARTICIPANTS TO FOCUS ON PORTIONS OF THE BOOK ASSIGNMENT THAT ARE IMPORTANT FOR THIS CLASS TO DISCUSS, ESPECIALLY AS IT RELATES TO THE MAIN PRINCIPLE.

III. Supporting Principles From Scripture—
Ephesians 4:26–32
Hebrews 12:14–15
Colossians 3:12–17

ENCOURAGE THE DISCUSSION LEADER AND PARTICIPANTS TO FOCUS ON PORTIONS OF THE

SCRIPTURE ASSIGNMENT THAT ARE IMPORTANT FOR THIS CLASS TO DISCUSS, ESPECIALLY AS IT RELATES TO THE MAIN PRINCIPLE.

A. Ephesians 4:26–32

1. God created the emotion of anger and it is not in itself sinful. The misuse of it is what God condemns. Do not allow your anger to be unresolved for even one day. When we go to bed with unresolved anger towards our mate, it gives the enemy a foothold in his attempt to destroy our marriages (**verses 26–27**).

> Smoldering anger acts like a wedge in the foundation of a marriage.

---

2. Do not criticize or tear down your mate. If you criticize your spouse, you criticize yourself since you are one flesh, and you also grieve the Holy Spirit.

   Instead, speak well of your spouse to others and also to him or her directly (**verses 29–30**).

3. Avoid bitterness, rage, anger, brawling and slander. Because God had compassion on you and forgave your sin, you should cultivate kindness, compassion and forgiveness towards those who have sinned against you (**verses 31–32**).

B. Hebrews 12:14–15

1. Work hard to promote peace between you and your spouse (**verse 14**).

2. Forgive your mate for any offense as soon as possible, before it has a chance to take root and produce a crop of bitterness, hatred, resentment and physical illness in your life. The longer you harbor unforgiveness, the harder it becomes to deal with. Practice extending forgiveness right away (**verse 15**). For the Christian, forgiveness is not an option; it is a requirement.
READ **MATTHEW 6:14–15**.

3. The longer unforgiveness remains, the more it will fester and have a negative effect on your physical, emotional and spiritual well-being. Unforgiveness doesn't care if you are right; if you allow it to remain, it will harm you and your family.

4. Choosing to forgive is like opening a wound to clean it, so it can heal. The following passage from Floyd McClung's book, *Learning to Love People You Don't Like* may be helpful:

> Sometimes forgiveness is a process. If we have been deeply hurt, it takes time for the wound to heal. In this case forgiveness acts as a continual cleansing of the wound so that it can heal properly.
>
> As we think about a person who has hurt us or sinned against us, feelings of resentment and emotional pain well up.
>
> Then we must reaffirm our commitment to forgive them. It is not that the first act of forgiveness was invalid, but that an ongoing process may be necessary until we are completely healed.[1]

C. Colossians 3:12–17

1. Because God chose us to be His children, His Spirit urges us to follow His example. By our will we line up with His forgiveness for the sins committed against us, just as He forgave our sins against Him (**verses 12–13**).

2. **"Bearing with one another"** means forgiving your spouse's sins against you and choosing to continue to direct your love toward him or her (**verse 13**).

3. Forgiving someone who has offended or neglected you is not easy.

Fortunately, forgiveness does not depend on your emotional state; it is a decision you make.
Forgiveness is an attitude you choose to have in your heart.

---

4. It is not denying you were hurt or letting the other person "off the hook." It is acknowledging that God holds the authority for this person's punishment, not you. God will give you this heart attitude if you ask Him.

Forgiving someone can be done only by the power of the Holy Spirit. Forgiveness originates in God, but you have to allow it to flow through you. God will provide the appropriate feelings later. Forgiveness brings healing to your marriage relationship and allows love to flow.

---

5. God's love is the outer garment and finishing touch to a well-dressed Christian. This garment covers and holds everything else together (**verse 14**).

6. Let the peace of God rule in your marriage (**verse 15**).

7. Spend time reading and meditating on Scripture and ask God to help you integrate His truth into your thinking and into your married life (**verse 16**).

8. Worship God with a grateful heart, focusing on His blessings in your marriage (**verse 16**).

9. Ask Jesus to show you how He wants you to act towards your mate (**verse 17**).

IV. Discussion of the Assigned Article

ENCOURAGE THE DISCUSSION LEADER AND PARTICIPANTS TO FOCUS ON PORTIONS OF THE ARTICLE ASSIGNMENT THAT ARE IMPORTANT FOR THIS CLASS TO DISCUSS, ESPECIALLY AS IT RELATES TO THE MAIN PRINCIPLE.

V. Next Week's Assignment

A. REVIEW NEXT WEEK'S ASSIGNMENT LISTED ON THE COURSE OUTLINE.

B. ASK PARTICIPANTS TO LOOK UP EACH OF THE SCRIPTURES ON THE **"I AM"** ARTICLE.

C. REVIEW THE MAIN PRINCIPLE FOR NEXT WEEK'S LESSON.

D. MAKE DISCUSSION LEADER ASSIGNMENTS FOR LESSON 12: ONE COUPLE/CLASS MEMBER

TO LEAD THE ASSIGNED ARTICLE DISCUSSION. ASK THE CLASS TO PRAY FOR THEM AS THEY PREPARE TO LEAD THE DISCUSSIONS.

E. ENCOURAGE THE CLASS TO ASK GOD DURING THE WEEK FOR A SCRIPTURE OR A WORD OF ENCOURAGEMENT OR EXHORTATION FOR NEXT WEEK'S DISCUSSION LEADERS AND TO BRING IT TO CLASS. TELL THEM THAT NEXT WEEK'S LESSON INCLUDES A TIME OF PRAYER AND MINISTRY FOR THIS COUPLE/PERSON.

VI. Ministry Time

Since forgiveness brings healing to the marriage relationship, you may want to lead the class in a time of asking for and extending forgiveness.

A. Ask God to bring to mind any hurt caused by your spouse for which you have not forgiven him or her. Ask God to remove any bitterness, anger, hatred or resentment that may have taken root.

B. Ask the Lord if you have done anything against your mate for which you need to ask his or her forgiveness.

C. IF BOTH PARTNERS ARE PRESENT, GIVE THEM TIME AND SPACE TO PRIVATELY EXTEND FORGIVENESS TOWARD EACH OTHER.

IF ONLY ONE IS PRESENT, SAY: Ask God to provide an opportunity for forgiveness to be expressed to your spouse. Ask God to show you if you need to make amends for any past sin.

D. BE SENSITIVE TO THE HOLY SPIRIT, IN CASE SOMEONE OTHER THAN THE DISCUSSION LEADERS NEEDS MINISTRY.

E. BE SURE TO PRAY FOR THIS WEEK'S DISCUSSION LEADERS.

F. AT THE BEGINNING OF THE MINISTRY TIME REMIND PARTICIPANTS ABOUT THE FOLLOWING:

As we minister to each other, we need to recognize that we are all fine-tuning our hearing of God's voice. We may not hear clearly all the time, so we need to carefully weigh any word of prophecy a class member gives us. The following is a helpful guideline:

If it doesn't make sense, put it on the shelf. If it contradicts what God has told you, let it drop. If your spirit confirms it, make a note of it in your journal and watch God bring it about.

G. ENCOURAGE HANDS-ON MINISTRY BY CLASS MEMBERS. ALLOW THE GIFTS OF THE SPIRIT TO MANIFEST IN DIFFERENT PEOPLE.

H. BE CAREFUL THAT ONE PERSON DOES NOT DOMINATE THE MINISTERING.

I. CLOSE WITH PRAYER.

IN MARRIAGE

LESSON 11

HOW TO SAVE YOUR MARRIAGE ALONE

MAIN PRINCIPLE

A marriage can be saved, even if it has only one partner who is willing to save it. Godly spouses are promised blessings from the Lord. God can empower us to become the husband or wife He wants us to be.

WWW.ZOEMINISTRIES.ORG

LESSON 11

How To Save Your Marriage Alone

I. Let's Get Started!

   A. WELCOME THE CLASS AND ENCOURAGE PARTICIPANTS TO SHARE WHAT GOD HAS BEEN DOING IN THEIR LIVES IN THE PAST WEEK.

   B. OPEN WITH PRAYER.

   C. WORSHIP THE LORD.

   D. HAVE SOMEONE READ THE MAIN PRINCIPLE FOR TODAY'S LESSON.

II. Supporting Principles From the Book

ENCOURAGE THE DISCUSSION LEADER AND PARTICIPANTS TO FOCUS ON PORTIONS OF THE BOOK ASSIGNMENT THAT ARE IMPORTANT FOR THIS CLASS TO DISCUSS, ESPECIALLY AS IT RELATES TO THE MAIN PRINCIPLE.

III. Supporting Principles From Scripture—1 Peter 3:1–12

AS DIRECTED, A FACILITATOR WILL NEED TO READ THE PASSAGE IN **APPENDIX A**. OTHERWISE, ENCOURAGE THE DISCUSSION LEADER AND PARTICIPANTS TO FOCUS ON PORTIONS OF THE

Lesson 11 — How To Save Your Marriage Alone

SCRIPTURE ASSIGNMENT THAT ARE IMPORTANT FOR THIS CLASS TO DISCUSS, ESPECIALLY AS IT RELATES TO THE MAIN PRINCIPLE.

A. **1 Peter 3:1–7**

READ **1 PETER 3:1–12** FROM *THE MESSAGE* FOUND IN **APPENDIX A**.

1. Eight ways to win a husband to God are found in **verses 1–6**.

    a. Submit to and obey your husband (**verse 1**). We can be submissive without being a doormat. Yandian in his book, *One Flesh*, says, "A submissive attitude is powerful because you are showing your husband the unconditional love of the Father in the greatest way. Regardless of his attitude toward you, regardless of his faults or mistakes, you are treating him with honor and respect."[1]

    b. We should not submit if what our husband asks of us is contrary to Scripture. Obey the Word of God.

    c. If a husband will not hear preaching of the Gospel, he will "hear" the preaching of the purity of his wife's behavior. If the wife will conduct herself with gentleness and purity, reverence to the husband, and in the fear of God, the husband may be won.

    Verse 2 of *The Amplified Bible* explains that to reverence your husband is **"to respect, defer to, revere him—to honor, esteem, appreciate, prize,. . . to admire, praise, be devoted to,**

deeply love, and to enjoy your husband."

- d. Don't let outward adorning be your chief aim in life. On the other hand, don't be sloppy in your appearance around the home. Remember that you dressed nicely for him when you were dating.

- e. Let the inner woman be adorned more than the outer woman (**verses 3–4**). Read your Bible. Know who you are in Christ and know your role as a wife, then stand secure in your understanding. REFER TO THE ARTICLE **"I AM"**. All the ornaments placed on the outside are of no value compared to a gentle and quiet spirit. Let God's light shine from your face.

- f. Trust in God (**verse 5**). Let Him meet the needs that your husband is not meeting. Let Him fill you with joy and this will make you beautiful in God's eyes.

- g. Do what is right and do not let fear influence your behavior (**verse 6**).

2. Two commands for husbands:

    a. Be considerate towards your wife. Give her no reason to sin. *The King James Version* reads,

    "Likewise, ye husbands, dwell with them according to knowledge . . ." verse 7. Yandian writes:

    > In this verse of Scripture . . . the Greek word for 'knowledge' is *gnosis*—simple, everyday knowledge . . . I don't know if a man can

ever fully understand his wife, but even a little knowledge of her can help him to be understanding . . . How is your wife like other women? Yet, how is she unique? What pleases her and what irritates her? What does she enjoy doing? What are her weaknesses, and how can you help her overcome them? What are her strengths, and how can you enhance them? Study her, talk to her, and observe how she reacts to different people and situations.[2]

  b. Recognize your wife as physically weaker, but respect her as a joint-heir with you of the grace of life, so that **"your prayers may not be hindered and cut off. [Otherwise you cannot pray effectively]" verse 7 (AMP)**.

B. **1 Peter 3:8-12**

  1. **Verses 8–11** concern the relationship of Christian brothers and sisters, but they can also be applied to marriage relationships as well.

    a. **"Finally, all [of you] should be of one and the same mind [united in spirit] . . ." verse 8 (AMP).**

    b. Sympathize with one another.

    c. Love one another with *phileo* love.

    d. Be compassionate and courteous (tenderhearted and humble) (**verse 8 AMP**).

    e. No revenge allowed (**verse 9**).

How To Hear God's Voice—In Marriage

    f. Bless your spouse, **". . . praying for their welfare, happiness and protection, and truly pitying them and loving them" verse 9 (AMP)**.

    g. Keep your tongue free from evil and your lips free from deceitful speech (**verse 10**).

    h. Turn away from evil and do good (**verse 11**).

2. **Verse 12** lists three blessings for the righteous. They are blessings for those who desire to be godly mates and have godly marriages:

    a. The eyes of the Lord will be upon you; He knows what you are going through.

    b. His ears are attentive to your prayer.

    c. His face is against your enemies, **"to oppose them, to frustrate and defeat them" verse 12 (AMP)**.

IV. Discussion of the Assigned Articles

ENCOURAGE THE DISCUSSION LEADER AND PARTICIPANTS TO FOCUS ON PORTIONS OF THE ARTICLE ASSIGNMENT THAT ARE IMPORTANT FOR THIS CLASS TO DISCUSS, ESPECIALLY AS IT RELATES TO THE MAIN PRINCIPLE.

V. How to Save Your Marriage Alone

IF YOU HAVE PARTICIPANTS IN YOUR CLASS WHO ARE TAKING THIS COURSE WITHOUT THEIR SPOUSE, ASK EACH ONE TO SHARE WHAT GUIDANCE GOD HAS GIVEN THEM REGARDING HOW THEY ARE TO PROCEED IN THEIR RELATIONSHIPS WITH GOD AND THEIR SPOUSE.

VI. Next Week's Assignment

A. REVIEW NEXT WEEK'S ASSIGNMENT LISTED ON THE COURSE OUTLINE.

B. ASK COUPLES TO LOOK AT THE LESSON 12 STUDY HELP **"SERVING GOD TOGETHER"** NOW. ASK IF THEY HAVE ANY QUESTIONS ABOUT THIS ASSIGNMENT.

C. REVIEW THE MAIN PRINCIPLE FOR NEXT WEEK'S LESSON.

D. MAKE DISCUSSION LEADER ASSIGNMENTS FOR LESSON 12: ONE COUPLE/CLASS MEMBER TO LEAD THE ASSIGNED ARTICLE DISCUSSION. ASK THE CLASS TO PRAY FOR THEM AS THEY PREPARE TO LEAD THE DISCUSSION.

E. ENCOURAGE THE CLASS TO ASK GOD DURING THE WEEK FOR A SCRIPTURE OR A WORD OF ENCOURAGEMENT OR EXHORTATION FOR NEXT WEEK'S DISCUSSION LEADERS AND TO BRING IT TO CLASS. TELL THEM THAT NEXT

WEEK'S LESSON INCLUDES A TIME OF PRAYER AND MINISTRY FOR THIS COUPLE/PERSON.

VII. Ministry Time

   A. AS FACILITATOR, YOU NEED TO GUIDE THE MINISTRY TIME.

   B. BE SURE TO PRAY FOR THIS WEEK'S DISCUSSION LEADERS.

   C. IN ADDITION, BE SENSITIVE TO THE NEEDS OF PARTICIPANTS WHO ARE TAKING THIS COURSE WITHOUT A SPOUSE. IF YOU SENSE THE LORD DIRECTING YOU TO ADDRESS THE NEED FOR MINISTRY IN A CLASS MEMBER, ASK THE PERSON CONCERNED IF HE OR SHE WOULD LIKE PRAYER.

   D. AT THE BEGINNING OF THE MINISTRY TIME REMIND PARTICIPANTS ABOUT THE FOLLOWING:

As we minister to each other, we need to recognize that we are all fine-tuning our hearing of God's voice. We may not hear clearly all the time, so we need to carefully weigh any word of prophecy a class member gives us. The following is a helpful guideline:

If it doesn't make sense, put it on the shelf. If it contradicts what God has told you, let it drop. If your spirit confirms it, make a note of it in your journal and watch God bring it about.

E. ENCOURAGE HANDS-ON MINISTRY BY CLASS MEMBERS. ALLOW THE GIFTS OF THE SPIRIT TO MANIFEST IN DIFFERENT PEOPLE.

F. BE CAREFUL THAT ONE PERSON DOES NOT DOMINATE THE MINISTERING.

G. CLOSE WITH PRAYER.

IN MARRIAGE

LESSON 12

SERVING GOD TOGETHER

MAIN PRINCIPLE

God has a plan for our marriage and shared ministry. God will reveal His plan for us as we walk in the Spirit together. He can empower us to become the husband or wife He wants us to be.

WWW.ZOEMINISTRIES.ORG

LESSON 12

Serving God Together

I. Let's Get Started!

A. WELCOME THE CLASS AND ENCOURAGE PARTICIPANTS TO SHARE WHAT GOD HAS BEEN DOING IN THEIR LIVES IN THE PAST WEEK.

B. OPEN WITH PRAYER.

C. WORSHIP THE LORD.

D. HAVE SOMEONE READ THE MAIN PRINCIPLE FOR TODAY'S LESSON.

II. "Serving God Together" Study Help

The goal of examining a couple in the Bible and their ministry is to help establish in our hearts what God has for each of us as a couple and in ministry.

A. **Question #1—Do a character study of a couple found in Scripture. Read between the lines of scripture and imagine what principles motivated your chosen Bible couple. Be ready to share the principles by which you think this couple lived and ministered together.**

1. ASK EACH COUPLE TO SHARE WITH THE CLASS ABOUT THE BIBLE COUPLE THEY CHOSE.

2. The following Scripture study will give you an idea of what you, as facilitator, might draw out of each couple. This study is on Aquila and Priscilla and can help you facilitate a discussion should class members choose this couple.

- **Acts 18:2–26**
- **Romans 16:3–4**
- **1 Corinthians 16:19**
- **2 Timothy 4:19**

Priscilla and Aquila were important missionaries in Corinth and Ephesus. Together they ministered God's word, established a church in their home, and were acknowledged as great servants of God by Paul and the author of Acts.

a. *They formed an effective team.*
   Their united efforts impacted those around them. They must have honored each other by allowing their individual strengths to complement each other (**Romans 16:3–4; 1 Corinthians 16:19**).

b. *They were committed to one another as covenant partners.*
   They were never mentioned apart from one another in the Bible. In marriage and ministry, they were always together. They must have loved each other deeply (**2 Timothy 4:19; Acts 18:2– 26**).

c. *They possessed a single mind and spirit.*
   Whatever they did, whether tent making, ministering at home or assuming leadership in the church at Ephesus or Corinth, they were of the same mind. This unity existed despite diverse traditions (Priscilla of Roman origin, and Aquila

of Hebrew origin) and probably diverse giftings. They went to Corinth, then to Ephesus, to Rome and finally back to Ephesus. They moved together under the direction of the Holy Spirit. They probably did not give place to jealousy, envy, selfishness or strife (**Acts 18:2–3,18–19; 1 Corinthians 16:19**).

d. *They made the most of their spiritual education.*
They listened carefully to sermons and evaluated what they learned. They were probably teachable. When they heard Apollos speak, they were impressed by his ability as an orator, but realized that the content of his message was not complete. Instead of open confrontation, the couple sensitively took Apollos home and shared with him what he needed to know. Until then, Apollos had only known John the Baptist's message about Christ. Priscilla and Aquila told him about Jesus' life, death and resurrection, and the reality of God's indwelling Spirit. Apollos continued to preach powerfully—but now with the full story and anointing because of their willingness to share what they knew (**Acts 18:24–26**).

e. *They were willing to serve God even unto death.*
Not only were they willing to crucify the flesh, but they risked their lives for Paul and other believers (**Romans 16:3**).

3. AFTER EACH COUPLE HAS SHARED THEIR SCRIPTURE STUDY OF A BIBLE COUPLE, ASK THE CLASS TO REFLECT ON THE CHARACTERISTICS OF ALL THE PEOPLE STUDIED.

Ask yourselves, "How do we measure up in our marriage, ministry and relationships?"

ENCOURAGE PARTICIPANTS TO SHARE THEIR THOUGHTS.

B. Question #2—Identify biblical principles by which you think God is asking you to live as a couple serving Him together in the future.

ASK EACH COUPLE TO SHARE WHAT THE BIBLICAL PRINCIPLES ARE THAT WILL FORM THE FOUNDATION OF THEIR SERVING GOD TOGETHER.

III. Discussion of the Assigned Article

ENCOURAGE THE DISCUSSION LEADER AND PARTICIPANTS TO FOCUS ON PORTIONS OF THE ARTICLE ASSIGNMENT THAT ARE IMPORTANT FOR THIS CLASS TO DISCUSS, ESPECIALLY AS IT RELATES TO THE MAIN PRINCIPLE.

IV. Supporting Principles From Scripture— 1 Corinthians 13:1–8a

A. READ THIS PASSAGE FROM *THE MESSAGE* FOUND IN **APPENDIX A**.

B. HAVE CLASS MEMBERS SHARE WHAT INSIGHTS THEY HAD WHILE READING THIS PASSAGE AT HOME.

V. Breaking Bread Together

As we break bread together, let this be a time of celebration of what God has done during this course.

A. A GLASS OF JUICE AND A PLATE OF BREAD MAY BE SET ON A SMALL TABLE IN THE CENTER OF THE ROOM.

Let us remember what Jesus did for us and appropriate all that his death provides for us.

B. HAVE THE HOST OR THE ASSISTANT FACILITATOR READ **1 CORINTHIANS 11:23–26**.

C. THEN EACH PARTICIPANT MAY PARTAKE OF THE ELEMENTS BY DIPPING THE BREAD INTO THE JUICE. THIS CAN BE DONE INDIVIDUALLY OR CORPORATELY, AS THE HOLY SPIRIT LEADS.

VI. Ministry Time

After breaking bread together, be sensitive to the leading of the Holy Spirit. Following are some suggestions to help you close out this course:

A. THE LORD OFTEN USES THIS TIME TO MINISTER POWERFULLY TO CLASS MEMBERS. ENCOURAGE THE CLASS TO WAIT ON THE LORD SO THAT EACH ONE IS GIVEN DIRECTION OR ENCOURAGEMENT, AS THE LORD DIRECTS. AS FACILITATOR, YOU STILL NEED TO GUIDE THE MINISTRY TIME.

Lesson 12 — Serving God Together

    B. THIS COULD BE A TIME TO ENCOURAGE PARTICIPANTS TO SHARE WHAT GOD HAS DONE IN THEIR LIVES DURING THIS COURSE.

    C. THE LORD MAY LEAD YOU TO CLOSE WITH A TIME OF WORSHIP AND REJOICING.

VII. Ending Note to Facilitators

IF CLASS MEMBERS EXPRESS AN INTEREST IN TAKING ANOTHER ZOE TRAINING COURSE, CONTACT A ZOE REPRESENTATIVE. A LIST OF ZOE COURSE DESCRIPTIONS IS IN THE LESSON 12 SECTION OF THE *IN MARRIAGE STUDY GUIDE*.

ENCOURAGE PARTICIPANTS TO READ ABOUT OUR COURSES ON THE ZOE WEBSITE AT: WWW.ZOEMINISTRIES.ORG/ZOE-COURSES.

ENDNOTES

Scripture quotations used appear from the following versions:
The Amplified Bible, Grand Rapids, Michigan: Zondervan Publishing House, 1987.
King James Version, Cleveland, Ohio: The World Publishing Co., Cleveland, Ohio.
Holy Bible, New International Version, Grand Rapids, Michigan: Zondervan Bible Publishers, 1988.
The Message, Eugene H. Peterson, Colorado Springs, Colorado: NavPress Publishing Group, 1993.

Scripture quotations are from the *New International Version* unless otherwise noted.

Lesson 1

1. [loyalty] *The American Heritage Dictionary of the English Language* (Boston: American Heritage Publishing Co., Inc. and Houghton Mifflin Co., 1969), p. 773.

Lesson 2

1. [zao] Joseph H. Thayer, *Thayer's Greek-English Lexicon of the New Testament* (Peabody, Massachusetts: Hendrickson Publishing, 2000), p. 270, #2198.

2. [stoicheo] James Strong, *Strong's Exhaustive Concordance* (Nashville, Tennessee: Crusade Bible Publishers, Inc.), #4748.

Lesson 3

1. [bara] Bob Yandian, *One Flesh* (Lake Mary, Florida: Charisma House, 1996), p. 4.

2. [Elohim] Kay Arthur, *Lord, I Want To Know You* (Colorado Springs, Colorado: WaterBrook Press, 1992), p. 21.

3. [brood] Strong, #7363.

4. [adam] Strong, #120.

5. [jatsar] Yandian, p. 10.

6. [asah] Ibid., p. 4.

7. [man's spirit] Ibid., p. 4.

8. [at conception] Ibid., p. 4.

9. [not complete] Finis Jennings Dake, *Dake's Annotated Reference Bible* (Lawrenceville, Georgia: Dake Bible Sales, Inc., 1963), p. 2, column 4, note r.

10. [his counterpart] Ibid., note s.

11. [meet] Strong, #5826 and #5828.

12. [from his side] Dake, p. 2, column 4, note z.

13. [woman] Yandian, p. 10.

14. [bana] Ibid., p. 11.

15. [he=Father] *The Interlinear Bible* (Lafayette, Indiana: Sovereign Grace Publishers, 1985), p. 2.

16. [proskollao] Strong, #4347.

17. [husband's example] Yandian, p. 89.

18. [respect] Strong, #5399.

Lesson 5

1. [Jewish wedding customs] Richard Booker, *Here Comes The Bride* (Houston, Texas: Sounds of the Trumpet, 1995), pp. 4-11.

2. [gird sword] Dake, p. 568, column 4, note 6.

3. [infrequent sex] Yandian, p. 151.

Lesson 6

1. [desire and character] Gary Smalley and John Trent, PhD., *Love Is A Decision* (Irving, Texas: Word, Inc., 1989), pp. 172-173.

Lesson 10

1. [forgiveness] Floyd McClung, *Learning To Love People You Don't Like* (Seattle, Washington: YWAM Publishing, 1992), pp. 55-56.

Lesson 11

1. [submissive] Yandian, p. 103.

2. [knowledge] Ibid., p. 79.

APPENDIX A

For Lesson 2:

Romans 7:25–8:14 (*The Message*):

"The answer, thank God, is that Jesus Christ can and does. He acted to set things right in this life of contradictions where I want to serve God with all my heart and mind, but am pulled by the influence of sin to do something totally different.

THE SOLUTION IS LIFE ON GOD'S TERMS

"With the arrival of Jesus, the Messiah, that fateful dilemma is resolved. Those who enter into Christ's being-here-for-us no longer have to live under a continuous, low-lying black cloud. A new power is in operation. The Spirit of life in Christ, like a strong wind, has magnificently cleared the air, freeing you from a fated lifetime of brutal tyranny at the hands of sin and death.

"God went for the jugular when he sent his own Son. He didn't deal with the problem as something remote and unimportant. In his Son, Jesus, he personally took on the human condition, entered the disordered mess of struggling humanity in order to set it right once and for all. The law code, weakened as it always was by fractured human nature, could never have done that.

"The law always ended up being used as a band-aid on sin instead of a deep healing of it. And now what the law code asked for but we couldn't deliver is accomplished as we, instead of redoubling our own efforts, simply embrace what the Spirit is doing in us.

"Those who think they can do it on their own end up obsessed with measuring their own moral muscle but never get around to exercising it in real life. Those who trust God's action in them find that God's Spirit is in them—living and breathing God! Obsession with self in these matters is a dead end; attention to God leads us out into the open, into a spacious, free life. Focusing on the self is the opposite of focusing on God. Anyone completely absorbed in self ignores who God is and what he is doing. And God isn't pleased at being ignored.

"But if God himself has taken up residence in your life, you can hardly be thinking more of yourself than of him. Anyone, of course, who has not welcomed this invisible but clearly present God, the Spirit of Christ, won't know what we're talking about. But for you who welcome him, in whom he dwells—even though you still experience all the limitations of sin—you yourself experience life on God's terms. It stands to reason, doesn't it, that if the alive-and-present God who raised Jesus from the dead moves into your life, he'll do the same thing in you that he did in Jesus, bringing you alive to himself? When God lives and breathes in you (and he does, as surely as he did in Jesus), you are delivered from that dead life. With his Spirit living in you, your body will be as alive as Christ's!

"So don't you see that we don't owe this old do-it-yourself life one red cent. There's nothing in it for us, nothing at all. The best thing to do is give it a decent burial and get on with your new life. God's Spirit beckons. There are things to do and places to go!

"This resurrection life you received from God is not a timid, grave tending life. It's adventurously expectant, greeting God with a childlike "What's next, Papa?" God's Spirit touches our spirits and confirms who we really are.

We know who he is, and we know who we are: Father and children. And we know we are going to get what's coming to us—an unbelievable inheritance! We go through exactly what Christ goes through. If we go through the hard times with him, then we're certainly going to go through the good times with him!"

For Lesson 5:

1 Corinthians 7:1–5 *(The Message)*:

"Now, getting down to the questions you asked in your letter to me. First, Is it a good thing to have sexual relations?

"Certainly—but only within a certain context. It's good for a man to have a wife, and for a woman to have a husband. Sexual drives are strong, but marriage is strong enough to contain them and provide for a balanced and fulfilling sexual life in a world of sexual disorder. The marriage bed must be a place of mutuality—the husband seeking to satisfy his wife, the wife seeking to satisfy her husband. Marriage is not a place to "stand up for your rights." Marriage is a decision to serve the other, whether in bed or out. Abstaining from sex is permissible for a period of time if you both agree to it, and if it's for the purposes of prayer and fasting—but only for such times. Then come back together again. Satan has an ingenious way of tempting us when we least expect it."

For Lesson 7:

Ephesians 5:21–33 (*The Message*):

"Out of respect for Christ, be courteously reverent to one another.

"Wives, understand and support your husbands in ways that show your support for Christ. The husband provides leadership to his wife the way Christ does to his church, not by domineering but by cherishing. So just as the church submits to Christ as he exercises such leadership, wives should likewise submit to their husbands.

"Husbands, go all out in our love for your wives, exactly as Christ did for the church—a love marked by giving, not getting. Christ's loves makes the church whole. His words evoke her beauty. Everything he does and says is designed to bring the best out of her, dressing her in dazzling white silk, radiant with holiness. And that is how husbands ought to love their wives. They're really doing themselves a favor—since they're already 'one' in marriage.

"No one abuses his own body, does he? No, he feeds and pampers it. That's how Christ treats us, the church, since we are part of his body. And this is why a man leaves father and mother and cherishes his wife. No longer two, they become 'one flesh.' This is a huge mystery, and I don't pretend to understand it all. What is clearest to me is the way Christ treats the church. And this provides a good picture of how each husband is to treat his wife, loving himself in loving her, and how each wife is to honor her husband."

For Lesson 11:

1 Peter 3:1–12 (*The Message*):

APPENDIX A

The same goes for you wives: Be good wives to your husbands, responsive to their needs. There are husbands who, indifferent as they are to any words about God, will be captivated by your life of holy beauty. What matters is not your outer appearance—the styling of your hair, the jewelry you wear, the cut of your clothes—but your inner disposition.

"Cultivate inner beauty, the gentle, gracious kind that God delights in. The holy women of old were beautiful before God that way, and were good, loyal wives to their husbands. Sarah, for instance, taking care of Abraham, would address him as 'my dear husband.' You'll be true daughters of Sarah if you do the same, unanxious and unintimidated.

"The same goes for you husbands: Be good husbands to your wives. Honor them, delight in them. As women they lack some of your advantages. But in the new life of God's grace, you're equals. Treat your wives, then, as equals so your prayers don't run aground.

"Summing up: Be agreeable, be sympathetic, be loving, be compassionate, be humble. That goes for all of you, no exceptions. No retaliation. No sharp-tongued sarcasm. Instead, bless—that's your job, to bless. You'll be a blessing and also get a blessing.

'Whoever wants to embrace life
    and see the day fill up with good,
Here's what you do:
    Say nothing evil or hurtful;
Snub evil and cultivate good;
    run after peace for all you're worth.
God looks on all this with approval,
    listening and responding well to what he's asked;

But he turns his back
   on those who do evil things.' "

For Lesson 12:

1 Corinthians 13:1–8a (*The Message*):

"If I speak with human eloquence and angelic ecstasy but don't love, I'm nothing but the creaking of a rusty gate.

"If I speak God's Word with power, revealing all his mysteries and making everything plain as day, and if I have faith that says to a mountain, "Jump," and it jumps, but I don't love, I'm nothing.

"If I give everything I own to the poor and even go to the stake to be burned as a martyr, but I don't love, I've gotten nowhere. So, no matter what I say, what I believe, and what I do, I'm bankrupt without love.

"Love never gives up.
Love cares for others more than for self.
Love doesn't want what it doesn't have.
Love doesn't strut,
Doesn't have a swelled head,
Doesn't force itself on others,
Isn't always "me first,"
Doesn't fly off the handle,
Doesn't keep score of the sins of others,
Doesn't revel when others grovel,
Takes pleasure in the flowering of truth,
Puts up with anything,
Trusts God always,
Always looks for the best,
Never looks back,
But keeps going to the end.
Love never dies."

APPENDIX B

Guidelines for a Personal Visit/Phone Call with Discussion Leaders

1. **Before the visit/call:**

   a. Set up a time to visit/call the couple/class member and tell them what the purpose of the visit/call is.

   b. Ask God what He wants to do in this couple/class member so that you will know how to pray for them personally. Ask for His guidance and protection during your time with the leaders.

   c. Look at the class material so that you will be able to answer any questions they have regarding the book, article and Scripture assignments.

2. **During the visit/call:**

   a. Pray that God would bless your time together and that He would bring to mind those things that need to be discussed.

   b. Ask how they are doing. Ask if they are enjoying the course.

   c. Ask if they have read the article **"Guidelines for Leading a Class Discussion."** Ask if they have any questions about this.

   d. Ask them if they have any questions about the information in the book, article or Scripture assignments. Ask if the Holy Spirit has given them any new insights.

e. Ask if they have questions to stimulate discussion.

f. Encourage them to be open to the Holy Spirit's leading as they prepare and lead the class.

g. Pray together and ask the Lord to anoint them for this task.

3. After the visit/call:

a. Pray for God's anointing, guidance and protection of these participants as they serve as discussion leaders.

b. Pray that God would continue to work in their lives.

www.ingramcontent.com/pod-product-compliance
Lightning Source LLC
Chambersburg PA
CBHW070912160426
43193CB00011B/1438